ABOUT THE AUTHORS

**Dr Kevin Dutton** is a research psychologist at the Department of Experimental Psychology, University of Oxford. He is an affiliated member of the Royal Society of Medicine and of the Society for the Scientific Study of Psychopathy. He is the author of the acclaimed *Flipnosis: The Art of Split-Second Persuasion* and *The Wisdom of Psychopaths: Lessons in Life from Saints, Spies and Serial Killers* as well as *The Good Psychopath's Guide to Success*. He lives in the Cotswolds.

**kevindutton.co.uk**
**thegoodpsychopath.com**
**@profkevindutton**

From the day he was found in a carrier bag on the steps of Guy's Hospital in London, **Andy McNab** has led an extraordinary life.

As a teenage delinquent, Andy McNab kicked against society. As a young soldier he waged war against the IRA in the streets and fields of South Armagh. As a member of 22 SAS he was at the centre of covert operations for nine years – on five continents. During the Gulf War he commanded Bravo Two Zero, a patrol that, in the words of his commanding officer, 'will remain in regimental history for ever'. Awarded both the Distinguished Conduct Medal (DCM) and Military Medal (MM) during his military career,

McNab was the British Army's most highly decorated serving soldier when he finally left the SAS.

Since then Andy McNab has become one of the world's bestselling writers, drawing on his insider knowledge and experience. As well as three nonfiction bestsellers including *Bravo Two Zero*, the bestselling British work of military history, and *The Good Psychopath's Guide to Success*, his first collaboration with Kevin Dutton, he is the author of the bestselling Nick Stone series and the Tom Buckingham thrillers. He has also written a number of books for children.

Besides his writing work, he lectures to security and intelligence agencies in both the USA and UK, works in the film industry advising Hollywood on everything from covert procedure to training civilian actors to act like soldiers, and he continues to be a spokesperson and fundraiser for both military and literacy charities.

**andymcnab.co.uk**

# SORTED!
## THE GOOD PSYCHOPATH'S GUIDE
## TO BOSSING YOUR LIFE

www.transworldbooks.co.uk

# DR KEVIN DUTTON & ANDY McNAB DCM MM

# SORTED!
## THE GOOD PSYCHOPATH'S GUIDE TO BOSSING YOUR LIFE

CARTOONS BY ROB MURRAY

BANTAM PRESS

LONDON · TORONTO · SYDNEY · AUCKLAND · JOHANNESBURG

TRANSWORLD PUBLISHERS
61–63 Uxbridge Road, London W5 5SA
www.transworldbooks.co.uk

Transworld is part of the Penguin Random House group of companies
whose addresses can be found at global.penguinrandomhouse.com

 Penguin
Random House
UK

First published in Great Britain in 2015 by Bantam Press
an imprint of Transworld Publishers

A CIP catalogue record for this book
is available from the British Library.

ISBN 9780593075579

Cartoons © Rob Murray 2015
Design and illustrations by Julia Lloyd
Typeset in 11½ on 15pt Electra LT Std
Printed and bound in Great Britain by
Clays Ltd, Bungay, Suffolk

Penguin Random House is committed to a sustainable
future for our business, our readers and our planet. This book
is made from Forest Stewardship Council® certified paper.

 MIX
Paper from
responsible sources
FSC
www.fsc.org    FSC® C018179

10 9 8 7 6 5 4 3 2 1

# CONTENTS

 INTRODUCTION

# PERSONALITY WITH A TAN

Hello, folks!

We're Kevin Dutton and Andy McNab – the unlikeliest creative partnership since Eminem and Elton John cavorted onstage together at the Grammys that time.

If this is the first time we've met, we'd better start by introducing ourselves. One of us is a psychologist at Oxford University. The other did nine years in the SAS and is now one of the UK's most successful entrepreneurs. If you don't already know which of us is which then we'll leave it up to you to figure it out. But suffice it to say that you wouldn't want to be standing behind McNab in the queue at Costa Coffee if they've run out of his favourite chocolate gold coins, and the last time Dutton changed a magazine was when he cancelled his subscription to *History Today* and went for *Architectural Digest*.

Oh, and McNab is also a psychopath.

Of course, if you *have* heard of us, there's a fair chance it may have something to do with a book we brought out last year called *The Good Psychopath's Guide To Success*. If books on personal development may be fancifully construed as deft keys of transcendental truth gently turning in antiquated, psychological locks, then *The Good Psychopath* was the mental health equivalent of a nail bomb.

In true Special Forces fashion, it blew in the windows of the self-help market and, amidst the burning rubble of popular acclaim, abseiled on to the roof of the UK bestsellers chart in a fireproof suit and a respirator.

Needless to say, when we say 'popular' we interpret that word strictly within the traditions of the postmodernist, neo-structuralist, symbolic interactionist school of semiotic analysis … the nearest approximation, in common, everyday parlance, arguably being '*un*-popular'.

At one point our Twitter account boasted more trolls than a Dungeons & Dragons convention in Tromsø and we had so many fruitcakes clowning around on our website that some bloke from Mr Kipling got on the blower asking if we had any spare.

'Talk about five a day,' Andy quipped at the time. 'We're on five *hundred* a day!'

Of course, we jest. The small facts that Companies House tried to ban The Good Psychopath Ltd when we first registered the name on the grounds of it being offensive, and that one senior clergyman took the liberty of informing us that we had about as much taste as one of Jeffrey Dahmer's TV dinners, were but mere trifles in the grand scheme of things. By return of email we respectfully pointed out to the eminent ecclesiastic that, actually, Jesus himself didn't fare too badly in the psychopath stakes – and as for his sawn-off sidekick Saint Paul … well, he made Ronnie Kray look like Peppa Pig.

Oddly enough, that seemed to do the trick. We never heard back from the maledictory monsignor.

Following its High Street smash-and-grab raid on the nation's assiduously assembled Popular Science window display, *The Good Psychopath's Guide To Success* continued to cuss and spit on the Kindle-lit street corners of erudite good taste and ended 2014 astride the *Sunday Times* 'Thinking Books' bestseller list. That this was due in no small measure to its being stocked by three of the UK's leading supermarkets – Asda, Tesco and Sainsbury's – and becoming, we like to think, part of many people's weekly shop is in little doubt.

Waitrose, it emerged, were also in the shake-up but it didn't work out. We pulled the plug when they refused to entertain the idea of a three-for-two offer alongside fifty litres of helicopter fuel and a case of Château Margaux 1966. (Note to the nine-year-old lad in the drinks aisle: No, son, 'lego' doesn't have a silent 't' like 'merlot'.)

For those of you who haven't read it – and you really should – *The Good Psychopath* outlines seven attributes of the psychopathic personality that:

- unleashed in the right CONTEXTS
- deployed in the right COMBINATIONS, and
- tuned to the right LEVELS ...

… can make you more SUCCESSFUL.
We call these attributes the SEVEN DEADLY WINS.
With good reason:

- there are SEVEN of them
- they're DEADLY, and
- they WIN.

# THE SEVEN DEADLY WINS

## 1. JUST DO IT

| IN THREE ... | PSYCHOPATHIC SKILL SET |
|---|---|
| 1. Lead<br>or<br>2. Follow<br>or<br>3. Get out of the way | Don't waste time over-thinking. Get it done and deliver with minimal fuss. |

### WHAT'S IT TO YOU?

Research shows that procrastination uses up valuable mental resources, and, a bit like leaving the lights on in the car, constitutes a subtle drain on battery power. So next time you find yourself putting off filing that report:

- *unchain your inner psychopath*
- *jumpstart your motivation*
- *toughen your resolve ...*

... and ask yourself this: since when did I need to feel like doing something in order to do it?

'I can honestly say,' comments Andy, 'that the only time I ever feel like doing something is when I'm actually doing it. The decision to do it is always cold and clinical.'

# 2. NAIL IT

| IN THREE ... | PSYCHOPATHIC SKILL SET |
|---|---|
| **1. Do**<br>or<br>**2. Die**<br>or<br>**3. Don't even try** | Commit 100 per cent. Switch on when it counts and play to win. |

## WHAT'S IT TO YOU?

In one famous experiment, scientists comparing the performance of psychopaths and non-psychopaths in a simple rule-learning game found that when mistakes were punished by painful electric shocks, the psychopaths were slower on the uptake. But when success was rewarded by the prospect of financial gain, the roles reversed. This time around the psychopaths cleaned up.

This ability to switch on when it matters is a trait common to psychopaths, top surgeons, leading CEOs and elite sportspeople (to name but a few professions).

Want to know the difference between the good and the great in sport? It's simple. The good get 85 per cent out of themselves while the great get 100 per cent. Count psychopaths in to that 'great' group, too.

# 3. BE YOUR OWN PERSON

| IN THREE ... | PSYCHOPATHIC SKILL SET |
|---|---|
| 1. Stand up<br><br>2. Head down<br><br>3. Crack on | Believe in yourself and have the courage of your convictions. |

## WHAT'S IT TO YOU?

If you were to put most of the decisions you make in life to a jury, 50 per cent of people would agree with your course of action and 50 per cent would disagree.

'Remember, you have the casting vote,' says Andy. 'You can't please all of the people all of the time. So why vote against yourself? I don't give a toss about what other people think about the decisions I make. I mean, why would I? There are people out there who think even Malala Yousafzai's an arsehole!'

# 4. BECOME A PERSUASION BLACK BELT

| IN THREE ... | PSYCHOPATHIC SKILL SET |
| --- | --- |
| 1. Make it easy | Study people, find out what makes them tick, and become a master in the art of social influence. |
| 2. Make it appealing | |
| 3. Make it personal | |

## WHAT'S IT TO YOU?

'I can read your brain like a subway map,' one of the world's top conmen once told me. 'And shuffle it like a deck of cards.'

Psychopaths are genius-level psychological code-breakers because, like any predator, getting inside the mind of their prey gives them a distinct advantage.

As my old man used to say: 'Persuasion ain't about getting people to do what they *don't* want to do. It's about giving people a reason to do what they *do* want to do.'

# 5. TAKE IT ON THE CHIN

| IN THREE ... | PSYCHOPATHIC SKILL SET |
|---|---|
| 1. Get up | Don't take rejection or setbacks personally. |
| 2. Get going | |
| 3. Get better | |

## WHAT'S IT TO YOU?

Focus on what you're good at – and do it. Avoid emotional hangovers. As Andy points out: 'Nothing is personal – even when it's personal! All it is … is *life*.'

Spot on.

In mock business scenarios, research shows that psychopathic negotiators make more money than other negotiators because they're way less bothered about being screwed by unfair deals … while in *real life* business scenarios, one of the defining traits of top hedge-fund managers is that once they've executed a trade, they concentrate exclusively on the next one, irrespective of whether they're up or down a billion.

I once asked Andy whether any of the things he'd done in the SAS – or subsequently, in the business world – ever kept him awake at night. He laughed. 'If you're the kind of person who lies in bed worrying all night,' he said, 'you wouldn't get anywhere near some of the boardrooms I've been in – let alone the SAS.'

As the Zen proverb goes: 'Let go – or be dragged.'

# 6. LIVE IN THE MOMENT

| IN THREE ... | PSYCHOPATHIC SKILL SET |
|---|---|
| 1. **Regret nothing** | Learn to stay focused in the here and now. |
| 2. **Fear nothing** | |
| 3. **Embrace everything** | |

## WHAT'S IT TO YOU?

'*Here's* where it's at and *now's* when it's happening,' says Andy. 'I mean, why the fuck would you want to be anywhere else?'

Bang on ... though, believe it or not, the ability to 'live in the moment' is something that psychopaths and elite Buddhist monks have in common. But whereas the 'saints' savour it ... the 'sinners' devour it. It's also another trait shared by top sportspeople.

Next time you're on your way to that crucial interview, remember this quote from the athlete Michael Johnson: 'Pressure is nothing more than the shadow of great opportunity.'

# 7. UNCOUPLE BEHAVIOUR FROM EMOTION

| IN THREE ... | PSYCHOPATHIC SKILL SET |
|---|---|
| 1. HOT tap<br><br>2. COLD tap<br><br>3. DOUBLE tap* | When it comes to solving problems, feelings are passengers. They deserve a trolley service every now and again but have no place in the cockpit. |

## WHAT'S IT TO YOU?

Guess what? Studies show that *imagining* making a difficult phone call is way more nerve-racking than actually picking up the phone and making it. So, whenever you're stressing over a difficult task, ask yourself this:

- *What would I do if I **didn't** feel this way?*
- *What would I do if I didn't give a damn what other people thought?*
- *What would I do if it just didn't matter?*

Or try this: 'Next time you've got a problem,' counsels Andy, 'imagine you're advising a friend on how to deal with it ... then follow that advice yourself. Take a step back, take a deep breath, and ... take the plunge!'

---

*A 'double tap' is a cool, calm and controlled shooting technique where two shots are fired in rapid succession at the same target with the same sight picture. It is used by the SAS in hostage rescue situations. Sorry, folks, but machine-gun fire bouncing off the walls and ceilings only happens when Sly Stallone and Bruce Willis are in the building.

Yes, on the one hand these credentials are the same as those possessed by your serial killers and corporate raiders like Hannibal Lecter and Jordan Belfort.

But on the other hand you're just as likely to find them in the steely, surgical stillness of a front-line operating theatre as in the mile-high boardroom of a ruthless, cigar-chomping asset stripper. The key to the conundrum is to think of the Seven Deadly Wins as being the dials on a psychological mixing desk which may be twiddled up and down depending on the circumstances.

Shunt them *all* on max, jack up the volume and guess what? You'll be playing back the soundtrack in a maximum security unit.

You'll be what we call a *bad* psychopath.

Someone who:

- *preys on others,*
- *is only interested in themselves, and*
- *has precious little sense of consequence, shame or remorse.*

Someone, in other words, for whom psychopathy is a curse.

But turn some up high and some down low when particular situations demand it and you'll be ripping it up in a different way to the Dahmers and Sutcliffes and Bundys.

You'll be, as we put it, a *good* psychopath.

Someone who:

- *doesn't exploit others,*
- *uses their psychopathic potential for the benefit of society, and*

- *assesses the needs of a situation and responds in appropriate measure.*

Someone, you might say, for whom psychopathy is a talent.

Here's another take on it from *Good Psychopath I*. A couple of years ago I visited Andy in Miami. He was there on a film shoot and one day we hit the beach. As we stood among the loungers sorting out our shit, some huge big fat fella yells at us from behind.

'Hey,' he drawls. 'Do you guys mind? I'm trying to get an all-over tan here!'

Andy turns to him and shrugs. 'Fuck me,' he says. 'That's asking an awful lot of the sun, mate,' and rolls out his towel on the sand.

You had to laugh!

But later it got us thinking … about the double-edged-sword nature of psychopathy. Sure, if you lie out in it from dawn to dusk psychopathy will burn you to a crisp. You'll have what amounts to personality cancer. But at low levels it's a different story. Take it a bit easier and psychopathy can do you good. It's personality with a tan.

And that's not all. Without it, just like the sun, we wouldn't be here in the first place. If our prehistoric ancestors some two hundred thousand years ago hadn't included among their number the ruthless, the resilient and the risk-takers, we would've perished, in an evolutionary eye-blink, on the Palaeolithic killing fields of deepest, darkest Africa.

# GRABBING THE BULLSHIT BY THE HORNS

Now as we said, *The Good Psychopath's Guide To Success* did all right for itself. Its no-nonsense bass riff got a lot of people's brains tapping. But when quite a number of readers began emailing in to tell us that, actually, although they got the general idea of the book, although they bought the underlying argument, they wanted just that little bit more, we sat up and started listening.

There were two main quibbles:

One was the level of detail. The other was focus.

For example, a lot of people pointed out that although the Seven Deadly Wins set out the general principles of the *Good Psychopath* philosophy, what was really needed now, alongside those principles, was a more practical user's guide as to precisely how they could be applied in everyday life … to achieve the kinds of concrete, common goals that all of us face either at home or at work, with friends or with family or with colleagues.

One reader pretty much summed it up for everyone, capturing the general tone of the feedback with a golfing analogy. You've introduced us to the clubs, she said. What we've got in the bag. You've explained the difference between a nine iron, a wedge and a putter.

But what you *haven't* explained is how, exactly, we use these clubs to navigate our way around the course … around the fairways and rough, the greens and the bunkers of life's tortuous 18-holes.

- I've seen an advert for my dream job. How do I ace the interview?
- I've just come back to my car and found the traffic warden reaching into his pocket. How do I convince him not to put pen to paper?

- My diary's a bag of bollocks. It's rammed full of shit I don't want to do. How do I say no to stuff?

When we began getting more and more messages like this, we decided to take up the challenge head on. To that end, we placed a link on our website inviting readers to tell us exactly what it was they most wanted help with. Not general help as in the 'How can I be more assertive?' or 'How can I stop putting things off until the last minute?' kind of advice. We'd covered that already. But a more specific kind of help for the specific kinds of goals such as those just mentioned. The instructions, to return to our golfing analogy, for playing particular types of shot in particular situations; for when to select one type of club over another – and how to use it – as opposed to broader, more wide-ranging guidance relating to the mojo, rules and object of the game.

The response was overwhelming and took us completely by surprise. Hundreds of people got in touch with plans, problems, challenges and conundrums they required assistance with. But one thing in particular caught our eye – something rather interesting that neither of us expected. Many of the dilemmas that readers sent in related not to success, as such, but to quality of life. Some were idiosyncratic, to say the least.

We wish the best of luck to the 19-year-old student who wrote in to ask us how she could break the news to her parents – both of whom were Jehovah's Witnesses – that she'd quit her diploma in Counselling and Pastoral Ministry and become a stripper in a Manchester titty bar. What could *possibly* go wrong … ?

And we give special mention to the Community Support Nurse from Guisborough who contributed the following screamer to the website:

Dear Good Psychopaths

I've been seeing my boyfriend for two and a half years now. He's a real charmer and turns heads whenever we go out but I just can't trust him. In fact, he's so untrustworthy I'm not even sure the baby I'm expecting is his!

(As Andy commented before passing it on to me: 'Note to Redcar and Cleveland NHS Services: keep her away from the family planning clinic.')

On the other hand, however, many of the messages we received tapped into similar themes …

- How do I get to spend more time with the kids?
- How can I get more out of work?
- How can I inject some fun back into my diary?

… themes which converged around three common objectives:

- How can I achieve a better work–life balance?
- How can I work smarter rather than harder?
- How can I improve the quality of my relationships?

So that was that.

'Why,' Andy asked, 'don't we write a book about:

- achieving a better work–life balance;
- working smarter rather than harder;
- improving the quality of our relationships?'

So we did!

In *Sorted! – The Good Psychopath's Guide To Bossing Your Life* we present the ultimate compendium to disarming life and getting *it* to do *your* dirty work rather than the other way around. Taking in all aspects of life – work, recreation, health, relationships, time management, those niggling little challenges of day-to-day living that each of us faces way more often than we'd like: how *do* we keep our inboxes at zero? – we offer you:

- *concrete*
- *practical*
- *step-by-step*

checklists to help you get more out of life than it gets out of you.

'People put up with so much bullshit,' says Andy. 'It's madness. Time to grab that bullshit by the horns!'

 ONE

# HOW TO ACHIEVE A GOOD WORK-LIFE BALANCE

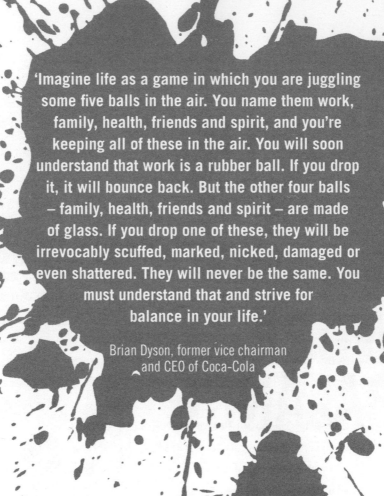

'Imagine life as a game in which you are juggling some five balls in the air. You name them work, family, health, friends and spirit, and you're keeping all of these in the air. You will soon understand that work is a rubber ball. If you drop it, it will bounce back. But the other four balls – family, health, friends and spirit – are made of glass. If you drop one of these, they will be irrevocably scuffed, marked, nicked, damaged or even shattered. They will never be the same. You must understand that and strive for balance in your life.'

Brian Dyson, former vice chairman and CEO of Coca-Cola

For many, a good work–life balance is as hard to find as Russell Brand in a biblically sized throng of Jesus-looking hipsters. But it was the Ancient Greeks who first put their marbled fingers on the problem over two millennia ago.

'Happiness does not exist in pastimes and amusements but in virtuous activities,' intoned Aristotle. 'It is a life which involves effort and is not spent in amusement.'

That said, however – and we doff our caps to the father of Western thought in all other respects – integrating your professional and personal lives in a way that allows you not only to succeed at both but *enjoy* both is not easy. Especially if you've maxed out the Barclaycard, run out of road with the overdraft, and pickpockets are slipping notes of complaint inside your Hollisters.

The figures on work-related stress are so depressing we pulled a sickie ourselves when we saw them. ('Who's *we?*' asks Andy.)

- **The total number of cases of work-related stress, depression or anxiety in 2013/14 in the UK was 487,000 (39 per cent) out of a total of 1,241,000 cases for all work-related illnesses.**
- **During the same period, the total number of working days lost due to stress, depression or anxiety was 11.2 million in 2013/14, an average of 23 days per case.**

So if for even one of those days *your* desk was vacant, then this is for you ... simple tips for getting some *life* back into your life!

# 1. GET A GRIP ON YOUR EMAIL

In April 2014 a spoof headline started doing the rounds that a law had been passed in France prohibiting all checking of email before the hours of 9 a.m. and after the hours of 6 p.m. It wasn't true, of course. It just tapped into our stereotype of the French being wine-quaffing, Brie-guzzling lazy bastards. But imagine if it was! Would we be any better off? There's evidence to suggest that we might.

Studies reveal that email is a significant provider of stress in the twenty-first century. It is the modern-day equivalent of the prehistoric beast that, in the days of our evolutionary forebears, constantly skulked around the mouth of the cave causing anxiety and uncertainty within.

Email, among other things:

- takes up, on average, 23 per cent of our working day (most of us don't just use it to communicate but also to track where we are on various tasks and projects)
- generates whopping great to-do lists
- necessitates multi-tasking
- (in many cases) decreases productivity
- activates both the reward and fear circuits of the brain (did you know that every time you receive a new email your cortisol level shoots up?)
- keeps us plugged into the loop 24/7

And that's before we factor in the emotional impact of some of the messages.

The penultimate item on the above list is perhaps the most damaging of all. Ever wondered why gambling is so addictive? It's because you never quite know when you're going to win. Such *variable interval reinforcement*, as it's known, exerts a powerful influence over our behaviour.

Anticipation is a bigger draw than certainty. We never know when the good – or the bad – stuff's going to come our way so we have to keep checking … and it's that occasional electronic pat on the back from the boss or, in contrast, that nagging feeling that the P45 might be on its way from *somewhere* that keeps us logging on for our regular online fix.

# GOOD PSYCHOPATH TIPS

## Get a Grip on Your Email

'Remember that twenty years ago email didn't exist,' says Andy. 'So cutting down isn't going to kill you. Here are a few simple rules that will help you strike a balance.'

---

### WHAT YOU DO

**Allocate set, predetermined periods of the day to go online**

### WHAT IT DOES

---

'Puts you in control of your inbox rather than the other way around,' explains Andy.

Which, judging by the figures, ushers in a much needed shift in power.

According to a survey conducted by AOL:

- 47 per cent of us claim to be hooked on email
- 25 per cent can't go without it for more than three days
- 60 per cent check email on vacation … and
- 59 per cent check it in the bathroom!

And these figures may well be conservative estimates. Another survey found that we consistently miscalculate the frequency with which we delve into our inboxes. On average, those who took part claimed it was once an hour. But when the researchers spied on them, guess what? It was once every five minutes.

Add to that the fact that it takes us an average of 64 seconds to recover our train of thought after responding to an email and that we generally allocate only 3 minutes to any given task before switching our focus to another, and it's easy to see how the most disruptive sound in the universe is 'PING!'

## WHAT YOU DO

**Impose a five-sentence cap on your emails.**

## WHAT IT DOES

Banishes the spectre of perfectionism.

'You don't have to write an essay every time you sit down at the keyboard,' says Andy. 'Plus, it frees up time to do other, more important things. You'll be surprised at how quickly people get used to it.'

He's right.

If it's any consolation, we consistently overestimate our ability to communicate effectively with email anyway. Especially when it comes to sarcasm. In one study, for example, volunteers thought they could reliably communicate sarcasm 80 per cent of the time. Face-to-face they were right. But over email they were way off the mark – the actual figure was 56 per cent.

Similar results have also been obtained with other emotions: anger, sadness, seriousness and humour.

Why else do you think we have emoticons? ☺

## WHAT YOU DO

**If something needs a long explanation, pick up the telephone**

## WHAT IT DOES

Saves time but also allows you to personally connect with the person on the other end – an essential aid to rapport-building.

One of the big problems with email is that electronic distance can often equate to emotional distance and negativity can set in very easily. Compared with face-to-face negotiations, for instance, people are not only less cooperative over email, they actually feel more justified in being less cooperative. The medium is so short and to the point that rapport is virtually non-existent, so if communication stalls it can quickly disintegrate.

Case in point: performance appraisals which are delivered over email are rated as considerably less flattering than pen-and-paper evaluations.

## WHAT YOU DO

**Have a pre-set selection of greetings and signatures that best suit your: name, affiliation, relationship with the recipient of your message and nature of the email**

## WHAT IT DOES

You'd be amazed at how much time you spend typing 'Hope you're well' and 'All the best' …

'Take a lesson out of the TV chef's book,' says Andy. '"Here's one I made earlier!"'

## WHAT YOU DO

**Don't keep re-reading and tweaking an email after you've written it.
Give it a quick once-over, then hit Send**

## WHAT IT DOES

Again, saves time, energy and sanity … and shows you haven't agonized over your response. Andy: 'If I get an email that looks really pimped I instantly get suspicious!'

## WHAT YOU DO

**SORT – treat email like you would regular mail**

## WHAT IT DOES

With your email divided into specific folders, you spend far less time trawling down the list trying to locate the details of that elusive product launch you were invited to last month.

Include 'Waiting For' as one of your folders. Once you've sent an email that requires a response, BCC yourself and drag it in. Check regularly to stay on top of the job.

## WHAT YOU DO

**Don't leave it … respond!**

## WHAT IT DOES

How much of your inbox is made up of emails that you 'put off until later' but still haven't got round to answering?

'If it was food in the fridge, you would've slung it out weeks ago,' says Andy. 'So why should this be any different? Stale emails smell just as bad. As soon as I sit down at my computer I have a two-step plan:

- *find, then*
- *respond or delete*

'Simple as that.'

# 2. SAY NO

If there's one thing we can learn from a two-year-old, it's the power of saying no. Try strapping an infant into a child seat when they don't fancy it and you'll know what we mean. As we get older, however, things get trickier. Before we know it, we begin to care far more about how other people feel than how we do, and are working around the clock because we've bitten off more than we can chew.

'We hate saying no because we mistake it for something else,' says Andy. 'We mistake it for negativity, a kind of default personality style that pisses on other people's parades. But "no" isn't something that defines who you are in general. It defines who you are *at a particular moment in time*. It's a clear choice, which by its very nature is going to surgically remove you from others. That's why it's painful.'

Andy's hunch is backed up by neuroscience. The brain, it turns out, has what we call a *negativity bias*. EEG studies of neural activity show that rejection triggers a tsunami of electrochemical superwaves, whereas a compliment, by comparison, produces a few gentle ripples.

But if you can live with the pain of dishing out pain to others – 'Or better still,' Andy points out, 'simply get used to it!' – saying 'no' has distinct benefits:

- It allows you, not others, to control your schedule.
- It allows you to pursue your own goals and agenda.
- It makes people sit up and take notice – and be more respectful of your time.
- It boosts your self-confidence.
- It transforms you from push-over pleaser to decisive boundary-setter.

- It makes your YES more valued.
- It separates out those who genuinely care about you from those who are trying to control you.

'You'll be surprised,' Andy points out. 'Most people's reactions are nowhere near as bad as you think they'll be. Chances are you'll probably just get, "OK." Then again, there's only one way to find out ...'

# GOOD PSYCHOPATH TIPS

## How to Say No

'If a two-year-old doesn't have a problem saying no, then why the fuck should you?' asks Andy. 'What went wrong in those intervening years? OK, so it's probably too much to expect you to scream the place down next time the boss wants you to stay behind and assist with preparations for the away day, but why not try a few of these instead?'

| 'NO' VARIATION | BENEFIT |
|---|---|
| NOT THIS TIME. | DOESN'T PULL THE SHUTTERS DOWN COMPLETELY. JUST GETS YOU OFF THE HOOK ON THE ONE OCCASION. A GOOD STARTER 'NO'. |
| I'LL THINK ABOUT IT. | DELAYING TACTIC THAT ENABLES YOU TO AVOID SAYING 'NO' IN COLD BLOOD AND TO DECLINE LATER FROM A SAFE DISTANCE. |
| I'M AFRAID I CAN'T. BUT HAVE YOU CONSIDERED... | CUSHIONS THE BLOW BY PROVIDING AN ALTERNATIVE. SHOWS YOU ARE WILLING TO HELP. |
| I'D LOVE TO BUT...(E.G. I'VE PROMISED A FRIEND WHO'S HAVING A BIT OF A BAD TIME AT THE MOMENT THAT I'LL GO ROUND TONIGHT). | CONVEYS APPRECIATION. PROVIDES A LEGITIMATE EXCUSE. SHOWS YOU IN A GOOD LIGHT. *'BETTER IF TRUE — BUT DOESN'T HAVE TO BE!'* (ANDY) |

# 3. INCREASE YOUR EFFICIENCY RATING

Andy once told me a joke. In fact, he tells me a lot of jokes, but this one was memorable because it was actually almost funny.

A man walks into a restaurant and pulls up a seat at a table. As he sits down he accidentally knocks a spoon on to the floor with his elbow. A passing waiter reaches into his jacket pocket, whips out a clean one and sets it down in front of him.

The man's impressed.

'Do all the waiters here carry spoons in their pockets?' he asks.

'Why yes,' replies the waiter. 'Six months ago an efficiency expert paid us a visit. During his time here he calculated that 21.4 per cent of our customers knock a spoon off the table and suggested that by carrying clean ones with us we could save on our trips to the kitchen.'

The man eats his meal.

Later, as he's settling the bill, he can't help noticing that the waiter has a string hanging from his fly.

'That's right,' confirms the waiter. 'We all do. You see, the same efficiency expert also concluded that we spend a disproportionate amount of man-hours washing our hands after using the bathroom.

'So the other end of that string is tied to my dick. Whenever I need to go I simply pull the string, let it all hang out, so to speak, and then return to work. I haven't actually touched myself so I don't need to wash my hands. Saves a lot of time.'

The diner is perplexed.

'But hang on a minute,' he protests. 'How the hell do you get your dick back in your pants?'

The waiter smiles genteelly.

'Well, I can't speak for the other guys,' he says. 'But I use the spoon.'

We're guessing that many of you will have had the odd run-in or two with so-called efficiency experts like this – which is why Andy's joke borders on the humorous for once. Sometimes, quite literally, they take the piss.

On the other hand, however, most of us – if we're being honest – would probably admit that we could save ourselves a lot of time and effort by working more efficiently.

Cases in point:

- You're working off two computers, not one.
- Your desktop is a collage of Internet Explorer tabs.
- Ping! You check your email. Fifteen seconds later – ping! – you check it again.
- It doesn't bother you that you've got back-to-back meetings at opposite ends of town this afternoon because tomorrow you've got back-to-back meetings at opposite ends of the country!
- It's your other half's birthday at the weekend and you've been meaning to call up the restaurant. Probably full by now though …

Ring any bells?

'You know,' says Andy, 'it's not rocket science. The more hours you spend at work, the more hours *outside of work* you're going to spend worrying about it. But most people think it's the other way round: the more hours you spend at your desk the more you can enjoy life when you're away from it!'

He's right.

Recent figures show that:

- One-third of us feel unhappy about the amount of time we devote to work.
- Over 40 per cent of us are neglecting other aspects of our lives because of work.
- More than a quarter of us feel depressed (27 per cent), one-third feel anxious (34 per cent), and over a half feel irritable (58 per cent) when working long hours.

So ... what can we do about it?

# GOOD PSYCHOPATH TIPS

## Increase Your Efficiency Rating

'Give me six hours to chop down a tree,' Abraham Lincoln once said, 'and I will spend the first four sharpening the axe.'

---

### WHAT YOU DO

**Balance vision with realism: assess every aspect of
a job before you start it**

### WHAT IT DOES

---

Enthusiasm and energy are great but without wisdom and prudence to temper them these two attributes can be costly.

'You can have the fastest car on the road,' Andy points out, 'but if you're going in the wrong direction the only thing you're going to be fast at is getting to where you don't want to be!'

---

### WHAT YOU DO

**Make a clear checklist of what you want to achieve –
and when – before embarking on a new project**

### WHAT IT DOES

---

Reduces the risk of repeating steps, missing steps out or duplicating what others are doing.

## WHAT YOU DO

**Go with the flow – focus on one thing at a time and give that one thing your best shot until you've finished it**

## WHAT IT DOES

Prevents multi-tasking, which decreases productivity by tying your brain to a psychological rack and over-stretching it.

## WHAT YOU DO

**Communicate effectively with your work colleagues**

## WHAT IT DOES

People are often reluctant to ask for clarification because they're keen to impress and don't want to appear ignorant.

To minimize the risk of misunderstanding – and time wasted on the wrong brief – make sure those you're working with know the *what, where and how* of what they're meant to be doing before they start doing it.

## WHAT YOU DO

***Under*-promise but *over*-deliver**

## WHAT IT DOES

Over-promising but under-delivering is one of the oldest tricks in the book if you want to lose clients and put yourself under unnecessary pressure in the process.

'So,' says Andy, 'resist the urge to impress with what you *say* and instead let what you *do* do the talking.'

Finishing a job in seven days when the original estimate was ten days makes both you and the client feel great.

Ten when you said seven? Not cool.

## WHAT YOU DO
**Use the rule of three**

## WHAT IT DOES

- An Englishman, a Scotsman and an Irishman ...
- *Veni, vidi, vici* ...
- As easy as ABC ...

In humour, in oratory, in fact in pretty much every form of communication there is, the number three casts a spell on the brain. Three is the minimum number you need in order to establish a possible connection between independent items – and if there's one thing the brain loves, it's simplicity.

Three also works its magic when it comes to decision-making. Give a client a choice between three options and not only do they make their mind up quicker, they actually feel better about their decision than if you'd presented them with twenty.

## WHAT YOU DO

**Delegate to the right people at the right time**

## WHAT IT DOES

Guards against the martyr complex – the tendency to feel that you 'have to do everything around here' – and aids both personal and collective efficiency by allowing other people in your team to develop their own skill sets complementary to your own.

'But delegation has to be done right,' cautions Andy. 'For example, if one person on the team is fast, then you put them on the part of the job that will take the longest. On the other hand, give the person with the eye for detail the most critical part.'

## 4. LEAVE WORK AT WORK

Sounds simple, doesn't it? The very definition of a good work–life balance. Yet, according to a report in the *Harvard Business Review*, around 20 per cent of us take work home with us every day.

Just think about that for a moment.

Twenty per cent! Every day! Not every other day. Or once or twice a week. The figures for that are far higher. But *every day*!

'No wonder one of the senior managers who called us in to his company said he felt like he was being "waterboarded by work",' Andy points out.

# GOOD PSYCHOPATH TIPS

## Keep the Wolf of Work Street from your Door

If you're among this 'non-stop nine-to-five' 20 per cent who are running on the spot on the corporate treadmill, you may want to take a leaf out of Andy's book.

'Back in my Regiment days it wasn't unusual to spend ten hours on the Lines* practising all sorts of James Bond stuff,' he tells me. 'Hostage rescue (with live ammunition), street-fighting, pursuit-driving, even safe-cracking. When we were finished you can imagine what kind of a mood we were in – pumped up and ready for action. But instead of roaring off to swing through the windows of an embassy or two, we had to go back to our wives and girlfriends at home, cut the grass and find the cat. Not exactly what we – or they – wanted. Nearly everyone's house had a fist-shaped hole in some door or other.

'The key, I discovered, to *not* joining the B&Q club at weekends and patching up the plasterboard was to make going home a discipline as opposed to a chore. A bit like a diver needing to decompress when reaching the surface, you need to mentally readjust to the new environment you're about to re-enter.

'My personal decompression chamber was a seven-mile run – alone – in the woods just outside Hereford around the base. By the time I was out of the shower, the handbrake turns and Heckler

---

*Stirling Lines, the name of the SAS's base in Hereford.

& Koch MP5s were history and the next thing I'd know I'd be stopping off for a takeaway in my knackered old Renault 5.

'Didn't stop me being married five times though!'

Andy's self-administered decompression treatment was ahead of its time. Nowadays, executive coaches encourage employees in high-pressure jobs to view the journey home as an opportunity not to cram in more work or to sleep, but to psychologically reorient to the end of the day.

- *Read a book.*
- *Listen to music.*
- *Call a friend.*
- *Even meditate.*

If you can stick to it – if you can adopt the mindset that shutting up shop is, as Andy points out, a discipline; that switching *off* is just as much a part of the job description as switching *on* – then it's powerful advice that will save you time in the long run.

In the meantime, however, here are a few other things you might want to do.

## WHAT YOU DO

**At close of play, make a list of all the loose ends outstanding from the day that are still on your mind. Leave this in the middle of your desk for the morning**

## WHAT IT DOES

Means you don't have to expend valuable mental energy remembering them during your down-time. A recent survey shows that, on average, people spend 46.9 per cent of their time thinking about something *other than what they're doing*.

When they're at work they're thinking about when they're not. And when they're *not*, they're thinking about *work*!

## WHAT YOU DO

**Before you start work, form a clear and specific intention in your mind that completing the close-of-play list will act as a trigger for you to:**

- *save as Draft,*
- *close the diary, and*
- *shut down the computer*

## WHAT IT DOES

Research shows that coming up with a simple but concrete plan of action ahead of time significantly increases your chances of pulling it off. But for the plan to work it has to be tied to a particular behavioural event.

Formulate the vague intention to '*Leave work around five*' and you'll be there until gone seven. '*As soon as I've written the last item on my tomorrow list*', however, and it's a different story: you'll be down in the car park faster than a whippet with its arse on fire.

As Andy points out with characteristic simplicity: 'It's like a form of self-hypnosis. The trigger event is like the snap of the hypnotist's fingers. As soon as it happens, you're into a completely different mindset.'

## WHAT YOU DO

**Get out your contract and take another look at your job description**

## WHAT IT DOES

'This serves as a good reality check,' comments Andy. 'Are you still doing the job you signed up for? Or have you taken on lots of extra duties and responsibilities that either *aren't* yours and you shouldn't be doing, or *are* yours but your boss isn't giving you credit for?

'Sounds like something you learn in HR 101 but you'd be amazed at how quickly, once people begin a new term of employment, that initial job description goes sailing out the window. In most cases it's really just the undercoat. Two weeks in, and you've got every man and his dog coming up to you with umpteen pots of emulsion painting their shitty little jobs all over it!'

## WHAT YOU DO

**Start keeping a log of your work hours
for intervals of 30–60 minutes**

## WHAT IT DOES

Provides you with a complete ergonomic body scan, allowing you to identify the presence of both full-blown psychological carcinomas (e.g. perfectionism; workaholism) as well as less malignant anomalies, such as time spent surfing the web for Coldplay tickets or nattering outside on the pavement over a fag.

---

### WHAT YOU DO
**Become a gamer**

### WHAT IT DOES

---

Fiendishly clever research shows that symptoms of PTSD may be tempered by playing the video game Tetris right after experiencing a traumatic event. Sounds bonkers – but not only is it true, the logic is water-tight. Here's how it works.

On the one hand, biologists studying the phenomenon of neuroplasticity* have discovered that memories are 'consolidated' or laid down in the brain over a period of approximately six hours. On the other hand, cognitive scientists have demonstrated that the brain's capacity to consolidate memories is limited.

Put the two together and it follows that an intensive mental task – such as Tetris – should, if played in the ensuing aftermath of a bad experience, successfully compete with the formation of negative images and thereby disrupt the development of traumatic flashbacks.

Of course, this doesn't just apply to bad experiences. It works for any experience. So if the evils of work are preying on your mind and you want to keep them firmly on the other side of your front door, then why not get your tablet out on the train home?

'Who'd have thought it?' laughs Andy. 'A tablet to *block* memories rather than enhance them!'

---

*The ability of the brain to constantly rewire itself and forge new neural pathways as a result of changes in behaviour and environment.

# 5. REMEMBER: GOOD ENOUGH IS GOOD ENOUGH

The world's most handsome man decides he must marry the world's most beautiful woman so the children they produce are stunning beyond compare.

So he embarks on a mission to find his perfect soulmate. Not long after beginning his quest, he meets a farmer with three knockout daughters. The man explains the situation to the farmer and asks his permission to marry one of them.

The farmer is sympathetic. 'Well,' he says, 'they're keen to get married so you came to the right place. Look them over and pick the one you want.'

The man can't believe his luck and takes the first daughter out on a date.

Next day the farmer asks how it went.

'Not bad,' says the man. 'But she's just a weeeeee bit … not that you'd really notice … pigeon-toed.'

The farmer nods and the man takes the second daughter out on a date.

Next day the farmer asks how it went.

'Not bad,' says the man. 'But she's just a weeeeee bit … not that you'd really notice … cross-eyed.'

The farmer nods and so the man tries his hand with the third girl. Next morning he rushes up to the farmer in a state of great excitement.

'She's perfect!' he exclaims. 'Just perfect! She's the one I want to marry!'

So they are wed right away.

Months later the baby is born and it's hideous. It's the ugliest, most unsightly child the man has ever set eyes on.

Horrified, he storms out of the nursery and demands an explanation from the farmer.

'How could we, the world's most beautiful couple, have the world's ugliest baby?' he yells.

'Well,' explains the farmer, 'it might've had something to do with the fact that she was just a weeeee bit … not that you'd really have noticed … pregnant when you met her.'

The big problem with perfectionism is that it's all in the mind. Whatever you're striving to achieve may *seem* perfect to you. But how do you know you've covered all the angles? All too often you *think* you've finally cracked it only for something to creep out of the woodwork and change everything. All that hard work, all those hours trying to get it just right … for nothing.

Even if you *do* manage to achieve an exceptional result, the chances are you still won't be happy. There'll be *something* that ruins it. Something that makes you think you could've done better.

'Perfectionism is to self-esteem what Jimmy Savile was to child-minding,' says Andy. 'A complete no-no. And that's because nothing is ever good enough.

'Eventually it stops you stone dead in your tracks. You don't do anything because you're shit scared you won't get it a hundred per cent right.'

The irony about perfectionism is that, as a work strategy, it's far from perfect. It's deeply flawed. If you're serious about your perfectionism, you'd never become a perfectionist!

Perfectionism is cancer of the diary.

It's a time tumour.

The more time you spend trying to perfect one thing, the less time you have to get other things there or thereabouts.

'And,' as Andy points out, 'more often than not, the things you need to get there or thereabouts are more important!'

The Beatles knew this from their earliest days in showbiz. In fact it was probably *the* biggest reason why they were so successful over the years and have such an enduring legacy.

'How come you guys wrote so many great songs?' a gobsmacked interviewer once asked John Lennon.

'Because we also wrote plenty of crap ones!' Lennon shot back.

# GOOD PSYCHOPATH TIPS

## Good Enough is Good Enough

But it's not all bad news. If there's one good thing about perfectionism it's this: we've yet to meet a perfectionist who doesn't admit to being one. And we've yet to meet a perfectionist who doesn't want to change. So if by any chance that's you, here's a few simple ways of getting started:

---

### WHAT YOU DO

**Before you begin a particular task, make a deal with yourself to be average**

### WHAT IT DOES

---

A few years ago, the singer Robbie Williams went through a period during which, despite his iconic status, he suffered from stage fright. A turning point came when someone he met offered him the following insight: he didn't have to be out of this world every time he walked onstage.

When you're Robbie Williams, average was good enough!

Williams found the observation profoundly cathartic and never looked back – a common feature among perfectionists, who are suddenly made aware of the dichotomy between being 'good enough' and being the greatest of all time.

'The key is deciding beforehand,' Andy explains. 'It lies in being psychologically aggressive with yourself and consciously seizing the initiative. That way *you* take control of the situation and impose *your* will on the task rather than letting whatever it is you're doing dictate your mental state.

'Stick with it and after a few goes you'll find that being average actually feels great … and that what feels even better is when you start to notice other people "trying too hard". There's nothing more uncool!

'In the Regiment you're taught from Day One to be the grey man. To not stand out in a crowd. And you know what, Kev? Forget the licence to kill. There's nothing more liberating than the *licence to bore the shit out of someone!'*

---

## WHAT YOU DO
### Put the kettle on

## WHAT IT DOES

Napoleon Bonaparte once quipped: 'The reason I beat the Austrians is they did not know the value of five minutes.'

Horatio Nelson made a similar observation: 'Time is everything; five minutes makes the difference between victory and defeat.'

And it's true!

It's amazing what you can get done in five minutes … if you allow yourself to.

'And it's also amazing just how many five-minute periods there are in a day!' laughs Andy. 'It's good discipline, five minutes. Sometimes, I lay my boring paperwork chores out on the kitchen table – bills, expenses, that kind of thing – put the kettle on, and aim to polish them all off by the time it boils. It's a little game I've played for years, and I've always beaten the whistle.

'But it's also a great workout for the mind. Keeps you fit and flexible. Brain cardio, I call it.'

Good advice that, from Andy. Because once, like him, you start to get five-minute-fit, you begin, quite literally, making short work of everything.

So why not put the kettle on and give it a try?

'After all,' says Tea Boy, 'what have you got to lose? At the very least you'll get a brew out of it!'

## WHAT YOU DO

**Forget 'What's it all about?'**
**Ask yourself: '*Who's* it all about?'**

## WHAT IT DOES

'When we were putting in the miles for SAS selection,' Andy tells me, 'one of the sergeants on the training wing down in Hereford told us something I'll never forget.'

He said:

> If you're trying to get into the SAS to please or impress someone else, you might as well pack your bags and piss off now. Because you're not going to make it. Because there'll come a time when things start to get so hard that you won't give a fuck about anyone else but yourself. To get into the SAS you have to really want it. And you have to want it for you.
>
> Not for the girl who blew you out at the school disco all those years ago and who's still strutting her stuff to *I Will*

*Survive* across the dance floors of your mind.

Nor for the teacher who kept telling you you were shit and bunging you in detention.

You have to want it for YOU.

The words of that training sergeant have stuck in *my* mind, too. Because he was bang on. Not just about SAS selection, but about the pursuit of any form of excellence. Scratch beneath the surface and, unlike Aretha Franklin's sisters, perfectionists are never 'doing it for themselves'. Instead, they're always trying to live up to someone else's expectations. Usually from way back. Some parent or teacher who hovers over them breathing down their necks every time they sit down at the computer.

So next time you open up Keynote or whatever, just pause for a moment and ask yourself this: 'Who's *my* invisible taskmaster?'

'And then, when you've got the answer,' says Andy, 'tell them to fuck off back to wherever they came from!'

## WHAT YOU DO
### Get a friend to set a timer
## WHAT IT DOES

Simple one, this. But it works wonders. The key, of course, lies in the friend setting the timer, and not you.

So next time you're about to begin a piece of work, ask a colleague to pull the plug on you in half an hour or so (or an hour, depending on what's appropriate for the task) and then drag you outside for a coffee or something.

'They'll know the score so you won't want to invalidate their commitment with any of that "just another five minutes" bollocks,' comments Andy.

And he's right. That's the beauty of it. Go back to school and into exam mode. What was it they used to say?

'Fuck knows,' says Andy.

'Finish the sentence that you're on and then put down your pens ...'

Trust us! It'll hurt for about fifteen minutes. But that's *it*.

'But just to be on the safe side,' adds Andy, 'especially in your first few stabs at it, before you go for that coffee shut down the work you were doing and open up another assignment so that when you go back to your desk you can start afresh on something completely different.'

## WHAT YOU DO
### Make a plan and stick to it
## WHAT IT DOES

This one's even simpler!

'You know, talking about exams,' I say to Andy, 'you'd be amazed at how many students don't achieve the grades they're capable of, not because they lack academic ability or anything like that, but because of poor planning. And ironically it's usually the good ones. They know their stuff but the problem is that they can't optimally distribute what they know across an allotted three-essay/ three-hour timeframe.'

It's a tell-tale pattern. Essay number one is seven pages, took an hour and twenty, and is brilliant. Essay number two is seven pages, took an hour and twenty, and is brilliant. But essay number three is a couple of pages of incoherent crap crammed into the last twenty minutes … which brings down their overall mark into the so-so category.

Unbelievably frustrating!

If only they'd been able to draw a line under the first two essays just that little bit sooner and average out their talent, they'd have walked it. But they didn't. Instead, they spent time they didn't have on two over-priced questions early on and by the time the rent was due on the third one the bailiffs were knocking on the door and they panicked.

In the workplace, just as in the exam hall, ability and organizational skill are like Noel and Liam Gallagher when it comes to performance and productivity. One without the other won't cut it.

ABILITY AND ORGANIZATIONAL SKILL: LIKE NOEL AND LIAM

Which is why having a concrete plan in front of you – even one as simple as that on the next page – is so important.

'So you might,' suggests Andy, 'think of each day as an exam.

'Not only is it all about line-drawing, those lines help you divide your days into time-locked "problem" compartments, enabling you to average out your *own* talent most efficiently. Time is like peanut butter – it should be spread evenly. Or, as we used to say in the Regiment: By the mile, it's a trial. By the yard, it's hard. But by the inch, it's a cinch.'

|  | Sun | Mon | Tue | Wed | Thu | Fri | Sat |
|---|---|---|---|---|---|---|---|
| 06.00 |  |  |  |  |  |  |  |
| 07.00 |  |  |  |  |  |  |  |
| 08.00 |  |  |  |  |  |  |  |
| 09.00 |  |  |  |  |  |  |  |
| 10.00 |  |  |  |  |  |  |  |
| 11.00 |  |  |  |  |  |  |  |
| 12.00 |  |  |  |  |  |  |  |
| 13.00 |  |  |  |  |  |  |  |
| 14.00 |  |  |  |  |  |  |  |
| 15.00 |  |  |  |  |  |  |  |
| 16.00 |  |  |  |  |  |  |  |
| 17.00 |  |  |  |  |  |  |  |
| 18.00 |  |  |  |  |  |  |  |
| 19.00 |  |  |  |  |  |  |  |
| 20.00 |  |  |  |  |  |  |  |
| 21.00 |  |  |  |  |  |  |  |
| 22.00 |  |  |  |  |  |  |  |
| 23.00 |  |  |  |  |  |  |  |
| 24.00 |  |  |  |  |  |  |  |

IT'S ALL ABOUT DRAWING LINES! A SIMPLE CHART LIKE THIS ENABLES YOU TO 'AVERAGE OUT YOUR TALENT' ACROSS EACH OF THE DAY'S 'PROBLEMS' IN OPTIMAL MEASURE.

# 6. ABOVE ALL … KEEP YOUR DIARY INTERESTING

'Where are you watching the Costa Rica game tomorrow?' Andy asks, as we enter a pub decked out in full World Cup regalia. 'You can come round mine if you want.'

I shake my head and get a couple of pints in.

'I won't be watching it anywhere, mate,' I say, wincing into my glass. 'I'm running a bloody seminar.'

The look on Andy's face is a picture. It is to compassion and empathy what Cyril Smith was to hang-gliding.

'You muppet!' he laughs. 'Why?'

'I stuck it in the diary months ago, before I knew the dates of the England games. I've been thinking of putting it off, but …'

'But what?'

'But I can't,' I say. 'It's for a Procrastinators Support Group.'

OK, confession time. How many times have you found yourself in this position? A year or so earlier it'd sounded great:

- *trip on Eurostar*
- *keynote address*
- *generous fee*
- *more than adequate expenses allocation* …

Of course you're going to say yes, it would be madness not to!

But what happens? Before you know it, in some freak mathematical pile-up in the fast lane of quantum relativity, time has suddenly concertinaed into a month … and then scrunched itself up into a day.

And guess what?

- You still haven't written your speech.
- You still haven't been on to booking.com.
- You still haven't cancelled the visit to the kitchen showroom (and told your other half the bad news).
- You still haven't asked Enrique if he'll chair the quarterly sales meeting in your absence (good luck with that, by the way – he's Costa Rican!).

It's all a total fuck-up.

Just like last time. And the time before that.

And you've only got yourself to blame. How the hell do you stop this happening again?

# GOOD PSYCHOPATH TIPS

## Keep Your Diary Interesting

The answer, according to Andy, is actually quite straightforward. In fact, it all boils down to a very simple question he's been asking himself for years … ever since the publication of *Bravo Two Zero* turned his diary – and his life – into an elaborate Excel spreadsheet of board meetings, film shoots, speaking engagements and prison visits (one of these days they'll take a leaf out of the Iraqis' book and keep the bastard in).

I'll let him explain:

'Any time anyone invites me to do anything,' he says, 'even if it's a year in advance, I ask myself: WOULD I DO IT TOMORROW? Simple as that. Just five magic words. *Not*: Would I do it on some abstract, unspecified day sometime in the vague, indeterminate future? *But*: Would I bin whatever I'm doing tomorrow and go there and do this instead?

'Whenever I get asked to do something, I sit down and ask myself honestly:

- What are they paying me? Is it enough to fuck the missus over tomorrow and have her bending my ear for the next few weeks about getting a new kitchen in?
- How important is it? Important enough to hand that backstabbing dickhead Enrique my state-of-the-art Powerpoint tomorrow and ask him to save my arse?

- How appealing is it? Good enough to miss the Costa
  Rica game tomorrow?

'In other words, as soon as my inbox goes *ping* and I open another request, I mentally cross out whatever date is suggested and insert tomorrow instead. It's amazing how that one simple word clarifies and crystallizes everything. It's a bit like at school when you had this big, long, complicated equation and by adding an "x" here and a "y" there it just crumbled into something dead easy.'

'It's called factorization,' I point out.

Andy stares at me blankly.

'Yeah?' he says. 'Well, factorize *this*, geek! Ticket for the World Cup Final? Yeah, I'd bin the sales meeting tomorrow and let Enrique take the credit. Shit, I'd emblazon his name on every fucking slide! Filming with Scarlett Johansson in the Ice Hotel in Sweden? Fuck the kitchen, mate – where are my long johns? Workshop at the Procrastinators Support Group? Now what do *you* think? I mean, the clue's in the title, isn't it? They're all going to bail and watch Rooney and Gerrard instead!'

# TWO

# HOW TO WORK SMARTER VS HARDER

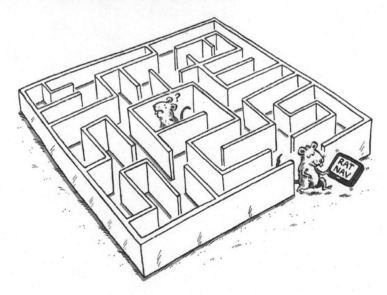

Busy.

Busy.

Busy.

Busy.

Busy.

Busy.

Dead.

'One of my favourite stories,' I tell Andy as we reflect on the day's events in the chrome, Pantone-splashed cafeteria of a company we've been called in to look at, 'is about the great nineteenth-century German mathematician Carl Friedrich Gauss.'

When Gauss is just seven years old, his teacher sets him and his classmates a problem. They have to add up all the numbers from one to a hundred. The teacher is satisfied that it'll take them the rest of the class, but after just twenty seconds or so young Gauss sticks up his hand.

'It's five thousand and fifty,' he says.

The teacher can't believe it.

'How did you get the answer so quickly?' he asks him.

The seven-year-old proceeds to explain:

$$100 + 1 = 101 \dots$$
$$\dots 99 + 2 = 101 \dots$$
$$\dots 98 + 3 = 101 \dots$$

'See,' he says. 'There's a pattern. From 1 to 100 there are 50 pairs of numbers that add up to 101. So the answer must be 50 X 101. Which is five thousand and fifty.'

Andy takes a sip of his customarily complicated, calamitously calorific coffee: on this occasion, a venti-skinny-red-eye-wet-latte-macchiato-with-four-pumps-of-syrup.

'I like it,' he nods. 'And you know what? The reason it's so powerful is because there's a lesson in there for all of us.'

'What – your coffee?' I ask.

He gives me The Look.

But fortunately this time, that's all.

'Sure, you'll eventually get there by going through the motions. By adding up the numbers. But actually, if you just invest a little bit of time working out the angles – working **smarter** instead of **harder** – not only will you get there a hell of a lot quicker, you'll be a hell of a lot happier when you do.'

Andy's point is a good one.

Here are some crazy stats for you. In the brief amount of time that it's taken you to read the beginning of this section:

- 6,400 mobile phones have been sold
- 1,100 computers have been produced
- 120,000 barrels of oil have been pumped
- 1,050,000 tweets have been posted
- 5,800,000 Google searches have been made
- 21,400,000 cigarettes have been smoked
- 300,000,000 emails have been sent

Moral of the story?

'If you've got an idea,' says Andy, 'don't fuck about. Crack on! Because somebody's already working on it!'

Scary, isn't it?

How many times have you gone the standard route – sat through the meetings, bashed out the presentations, ploughed through the small print with a fine-tooth comb – only later to discover that if you'd only done X before you'd attempted Y the whole operation would've been a damn sight easier?

If all this 'adds up' and you're starting to see some patterns of your own developing here, then why not try the following tips to shake things up a bit?

As Andy once told me: 'There's an old saying in the fight game, Kev. BIG beats SMALL. But you know what? In my experience, FAST beats both!'

# 1. PRIORITIZE

Stephen Hawking might be a master of Time, but the US President Dwight D. Eisenhower was a master of Time Management.

'If everything is an emergency, then nothing is an emergency,' Eisenhower reputedly once said.

'Good job he never joined the fire service,' says Andy.

Eisenhower also said something else:

'The most urgent decisions are rarely the most important ones.'

He was right on both counts.

In fact, Eisenhower's ability to get more miles out of a gallon of time than any of his contemporaries led to his being immortalized not just in Politics but in Management. The Eisenhower Matrix, which you can see below, is a brilliantly simple guide to structuring your workload. Stick to its idiot-proof principles and you'll get way more crap off your desk in way less time.

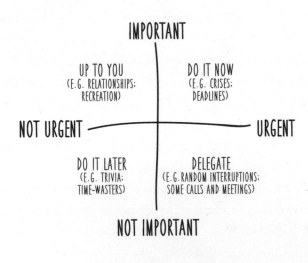

THE EISENHOWER MATRIX

# GOOD PSYCHOPATH TIPS

## Time Management

So, is that all there is to getting stuff done quicker and better? Well, not quite. QUICKER and BETTER are two short words with some bloody long science behind them. Here's a bit more:

---

### WHAT YOU DO
**Ask: what would Eisenhower do?**

### WHAT IT DOES

---

'I've met so many senior managers,' Andy tells me, 'who are what I call Time Dyslexic. If you think of letters and words as being hours and days then they get everything in the wrong order. They end up making one call when they should be making another. They go out on the piss with their "man on the ground" in Brussels when they should be wining and dining the EU expert on environmental law. All sorts.

'You'd be surprised at how many of them have trouble reading time. They've got a time-reading age of six!'

I like this analogy of being able to 'read' time. In fact, a friend of mine who is a primary school teacher does an exercise in her class that hands her bunch of unruly six-year-olds a lesson in time-reading that they never, ever forget – see overleaf.

# FAST-AS-YOU-CAN WORKSHEET

**Materials:** lined paper, pencil, crayons. **Instructions:**

1. Read all the way through before beginning.
2. Take one sheet of lined paper and place it on your desk.
3. Starting from the top, number every other line from 1 to 7.
4. On line 1, write your name.
5. On line 2, write the name of the person sitting nearest you.
6. On line 6, draw stars using a blue crayon.
7. In the centre of the paper, draw a box.
8. Divide the box into four equal parts with a brown crayon.
9. Colour the sections of the box in blue, orange, yellow and red.
10. Write the number of brothers and sisters you have to the right of the box.
11. Turn your paper upside down.
12. Write today's date.
13. Turn your paper the right way up again.
14. On line 3, draw a small picture of your favourite food.
15. On line 4, write a dog's name, either your own dog or someone else's.
16. On line 5, draw stars with an orange crayon to match those on line 6.
17. On line 7, write a word in capital letters that describes the weather today.
18. Draw either the sun or clouds below the box in the middle.
19. Fold the sheet of paper into four.
20. Write your name on the outside.
21. Ignore instructions two to twenty and enjoy watching everyone else do this activity wrong.

Just like normal reading, some of us are better at it than others and all of us stumble over the odd word or two every now and again. But if you want to be word – or rather, hour – perfect, there's a solution. Whatever job lands on your desk, immediately assign it to one of the four compartments in the Eisenhower Matrix and then take the appropriate action.

'And ideally,' Andy adds, 'you should begin each week with a clean slate. An empty matrix. Even the Not Urgent sections should be hoovered regularly.'

## WHAT YOU DO

**If you want to be good at business, you need to have a nose for it.
But if you want to be *really* good, you need to see beyond it!**

## WHAT IT DOES

'But I'm good under pressure. In fact, I'm *so* good under pressure that there are times when I'll put things off on purpose in order to create that pressure!'

Believe it or not, a senior partner in a top London law firm told us this. When we heard it we weren't sure whether to recommend him for therapy or have a word with a couple of our mates in the stand-up business … until we realized that there might be a pearl of wisdom in what he said.

For most of us, however, pressure is something to be avoided if at all possible, although, as you'll see from the figure overleaf, no pressure at all can be just as detrimental to performance: pressure, like everything else in life, has an optimal level.

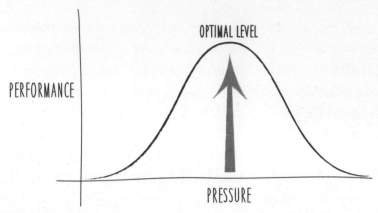

*Too much pressure certainly isn't good — but neither is too little*

'You know, when people think about the SAS, the first thing that usually springs to mind is blokes in black abseiling down from helicopters on to burning buildings,' Andy tells me. 'But actually that's just one aspect of the job – the *Urgent* and *Important* bit.

'There are a lot of other aspects that fall into the *Important Not Urgent* category which, if you do them in good time, can stop things leaking into *Important* and *Urgent* in the first place.

'Things like intelligence gathering, for instance. Or "hearts and minds": when you connect with local communities on the ground to gain their trust and bring them on-side.'

What Andy says is spot on, of course … and there's a lesson in there for all of us.

Most of us concentrate on stuff that's *important* and *urgent*: on stuff that has to be done immediately or else the customized number plate changes to P45. But start summoning up the discipline to deal with important tasks *before* they become urgent, to focus a little more on strategic, long-term decisions, and you'll find, pretty soon, that nice green spaces begin appearing in your schedule where previously it was all built up.

Of course if, like our lawyer friend, you really *do* prefer living in Time's bustling inner-city hour-blocks and getting snarled up in deadline gridlock every day, then that's fine. Just beware of the frequent property crashes in that cut-and-thrust, pressure-cooker neighbourhood.

---

## WHAT YOU DO

**20:20 vision codes for perfect eyesight**

**20:80 vision codes for perfect foresight**

## WHAT IT DOES

In 1906 the Italian economist Vilfredo Pareto made a startling observation: 80 per cent of the land in Italy was owned by 20 per cent of the people.

He also discovered something rather odd happening in his back garden: 20 per cent of the pea pods contained 80 per cent of the peas.

As one might expect, this rather mysterious distribution pattern began to garner attention and, sure enough, in recent years the so-called Pareto Principle has been applied to everything from business (80 per cent of sales come from 20 per cent of clients) to IT (Microsoft noted that they could eliminate 80 per cent of all reported computer glitches by eradicating the top 20 per cent of all recorded bugs).

Unsurprisingly, perhaps, the workplace also has some runners in the 80–20 stakes, two of which are as follows:

- 80% of tasks can be completed in 20% of the time.
- 80% of results come from 20% of the tasks.

The implications are clear as day.

'First,' says Andy, 'you work out which tasks make up that first 80 per cent – and prioritize them. You then work out which of the tasks in that 80 per cent are the same as those in the 20 per cent that produce 80 per cent of the results – and you give them *top* priority.'

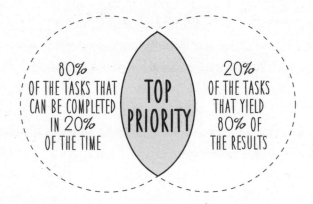

80%
OF THE TASKS THAT
CAN BE COMPLETED
IN 20%
OF THE TIME

TOP
PRIORITY

20%
OF THE TASKS
THAT YIELD
80% OF
THE RESULTS

There are a small, elite group of tasks which are Gold Card members of your work schedule and should be fast-tracked

# 2. ORGANIZE

Last summer Andy and I were having a couple of quiet pints along the river on the South Bank when, a few metres away to our right, some rat-arsed busker starts up on a violin.

Actually, let me rephrase that. *I* was having a couple of quiet pints. *Andy* was nursing what looked like liquid bubble-gum: a cocktail (I'll take his word for it) called a Shirley Temple.

Some months ago he decided to go on the wagon and in typical McNab fashion had strapped himself down so tight he made *Fifty Shades of Grey* look like crochet. I wasn't complaining, though. He was still good company. And this way I didn't have to tuck him in at night with his One Direction hot-water bottle and copy of the *Beano*. I could stay for last orders.

I digress. Back to the busker. He looked like Nigel Kennedy and played like Nigel Farage. *Not* a great combination. I'm not saying he was bad but if he'd been in the band on the *Titanic* the lifeboats would've filled up faster than Luis Suárez at an all-you-can-eat BBQ.

'You know,' I turn to Andy as the evening sun sets fire to the city up west, 'there was a study done a few years ago which looked at elite violinists like him. More specifically, at what separated them out from ... well, really good violinists. And one of the things they found was that—'

'They don't knock back six cans of Tennent's before they crack open the Chopin?' says Andy.

'*Apart* from that,' I continue, 'is that they don't practise *more* than the good ones but when they *do* practise they practise smarter. They practise in a more FOCUSED and – to use the technical term – DELIBERATE way. Oh, and they also get more sleep!'

Andy nods. 'That's exactly the way the Regiment operates,' he says.

'What, you mean you spend hours and hours working on different shut-eye techniques?' I smile.

Andy takes a sip of the pink stuff. 'Not exactly,' he says. 'But we're pretty good at shutting *mouths*, mate! No, in the Regiment you don't train randomly just for training's sake. You practise set, premeditated drills with specific goals in mind: in the CRW [Counter Revolutionary Warfare] unit, for example, room-clearance techniques in the event of a hostage rescue situation.

'I mean, you don't need to be in the SAS to work that one out, Kev. If you want to get better at something, you don't just focus on the stuff you're already good at. You work on the difficult stuff. The tricky stuff. The stuff that gives you the edge.

'And yes, because that kind of stuff takes more out of you than the easy stuff, rest *does* play a vital role.'

# GOOD PSYCHOPATH TIPS

## Organize
### ATTEN-SHUN!

'Do you know why the light that comes out of a LASER is way more powerful than the light that comes out of a TORCH?' Andy asks. 'It's because the photons that make up laser light are all marching in step towards a single, sharply defined RVP [rendezvous point] like a well-drilled army.'

'What, you mean like the light infantry?' I say.

Andy clears his throat. 'The torchlight photons, on the other hand, are like a load of pissheads coming out of a pub at closing time and heading for the kebab van. They're all over the shop, veering off here, there and everywhere. Well, our minds work in exactly the same way. Get all your thoughts together in step and in formation and assign them a clear RVP and you'll have laser-like focus that cuts through problems like nobody's business.

'But if every time you sit down at your desk you hand over your psychological credit card and let them go out on a jolly, then all you're going to have to show for it come five o'clock is the world's biggest hangover.'

Time for some basic training …

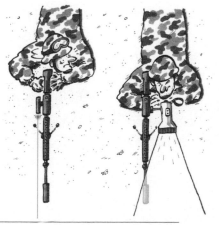

## WHAT YOU DO
**Don't just sit there … DO SOMETHING!**

## WHAT IT DOES

'I've started so I'll finish.'

So goes the catchphrase on the popular TV quiz show *Mastermind*. But actually that catchphrase effectively encapsulates a fundamental rule of human behaviour, summed up by what psychologists call the Zeigarnik Effect.

The Zeigarnik Effect refers to the intrusive thoughts that creep into our heads when we begin a task but subsequently fail to complete it. Often, we find these thoughts so aversive that, in order to get rid of them, we return to the task to get it off our mental desktops. In one study, for example, participants were given a load of brainteasers to solve but not enough time to do it.

Incredibly, 90 per cent of them went back to the puzzles after the study was over. It is, it would seem, human nature to finish what we start.

'Which is why,' as Andy rightly points out, 'we don't like to leave a movie halfway through. We want to know how it ends.'

Now, the Zeigarnik Effect is actually rather useful. We can turn it to our advantage. Ever wondered why you suddenly find yourself pretending to be purposeful – clearing out your drawers or reorganizing your DVD collection – when you've got something BIG and IMPORTANT to do?

It's because your brain is basically a scaredy cat. BIG and IMPORTANT bully it into submission before you've even started. And, like all bullies, BIG and IMPORTANT use threats and shows of strength to get you to do what they want – which is why, whenever you're confronted with a large project, you never imagine the easy bits and always visualize the hardest bits.

Bottom line?

'Just crack on!' says Andy. 'Because once you start you won't want to stop. Stand up to the bullies and you'll find they do a runner. But you can also make things a lot easier for yourself. Sometimes, in the Regiment, we used to invoke the GOD principle:

- **Guts**
- **Organization**
- **Determination**

'With GOD on your side you can achieve pretty much anything – though you don't always need the full Monty, of course. It depends on the situation. Here, for example, with a bit of *organization* you can stack the odds of getting stuck in early much more in your favour. So, the night before you plan to start the project:

- **Get everything together you'll need.**
- **Prepare your workspace.**
- **Sketch out a to-do list.**

'In other words, in the build-up to the project don't focus on your motivation for doing it. Focus, instead, on making it as easy as possible. Next thing you know you'll be halfway through.'

## WHAT YOU DO

**Treat each day like a series of Middle Distance events.**

***Not* a Marathon.**

## WHAT IT DOES

My old man knew all about the Zeigarnik Effect, I tell Andy. He had Parkinson's – and one of the problems with Parkinson's is that you have trouble initiating movement. But then, once you're up and running, you can't stop. The brain's on–off switch is buggered.

One day my old man's on his way to the shops when he sees a bus approaching. He's some way from the stop but, try as he might, he just can't seem to get his legs moving. The bus driver clocks him and, sensing that he might be in difficulty, slams on the breaks and grinds to a halt some fifty or so metres in front of him.

Eventually, my old man clicks into gear and, seeing him legging it ever closer in his rear-view mirror, the driver opens the doors … only for my old man to sail straight past.

'You piss-taking bastard!' the driver yells out as he eventually catches up with him down the road. 'From now on, any bus I'm driving, mate: you're barred!'

My old man gives him the V-sign.

'I can't fucking stop, you dick!' he shouts back, and continues barrelling on down the Old Kent Road towards Asda like Peckham's answer to Forrest Gump.

Andy is in hysterics when I tell him this story.

'Fucking hell, Kev!' he splutters. 'Your old man would've cruised SAS selection. But you know what? There's a moral in that story for everyone. Getting started on a task is one thing. Knowing when to stop is something completely different. And both are equally important.'

Andy, of course, is right. And there's science in the mix to prove it.

A study commissioned by the US Army's Research Institute for the Behavioral and Social Sciences showed that the optimal cycle of work–rest activity consists of 90-minute sessions interspersed by short cool-down periods of no more than 15–20 minutes.

This is the cycle that most closely maps on to our natural energy cycles – what's known in the trade as our ultradian vitality rhythm*– thus enabling us to work *with* our body clocks (rather than against them, as is usually the case) in maintaining focus and boosting productivity.

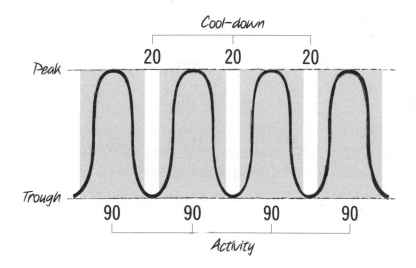

*Our natural energy cycle: how we can best use the minutes in a day*

---

*An ultradian rhythm refers to a cyclical period recurring throughout the day that is shorter than a day and longer than an hour.

Not only that, but it also corresponds to the most common practice regimen found among our elite violinists of earlier: ninety minutes of intense rehearsal followed by a quarter of an hour of downtime.

'At the end of the day it's a no-brainer,' says Andy. 'Top athletes don't train for six hours a day solid, do they? Instead, to ensure that they're getting the best out of themselves, they spread the pain across three sessions of maybe two hours each. It's basic common sense. It's much easier to commit a hundred per cent if you know there's a break on the horizon.'

So now you know. Don't run. Cycle!

## WHAT YOU DO
### Work clean
## WHAT IT DOES

This seems to be the section for tales about US presidents ... because here's another one, this time involving Calvin Coolidge. One day, Coolidge and his wife are on a guided tour of a farm. On entering the chicken yard the First Lady is taken aback by the rooster's limitless libido. He makes Tiger Woods look like Donny Osmond.

'How often does he do that?' she asks the attendant.

'Oh, dozens of times a day,' the attendant replies.

Coolidge's wife is gobsmacked.

'Tell that to the president when he comes by,' she says.

A short while later Coolidge hears the news.

'Same hen every time?' he asks.

'Oh, no, Mr President,' says the attendant. 'A different hen every time.'

The president smiles. 'Tell that to Mrs Coolidge,' he says.

This story, apparently true, is well known to psychologists. It has given its name to a well-documented psycho-physiological phenomenon known as the Coolidge Effect.

The Coolidge Effect – which, incidentally, has been observed across all mammalian species, not just footballers – describes what happens when a male is introduced to a shiny new sex partner having previously just … exerted himself.

He exhibits renewed sexual interest.

To a lesser extent it also explains why kids can't finish their greens but can polish off tub-loads of ice cream and why, after doing the accounts, we feel completely drained of energy only to miraculously spring back to life on the five-a-side pitch ten minutes later.

A change is as good as a rest!

Perhaps unsurprisingly, Andy has been cashing in on the Coolidge Effect for years. But not, he's at pains to point out, in the way you might think! Instead, he's used it to increase his productivity.

'I love writing in different places,' he tells me. 'I mean, literally: cafes, bookshops, bistros … and because I'm a ghost, because no one knows who I am, no one ever bothers me. So in the morning, on a writing day, I'll take the laptop into town, sit in a cafe and order a coffee, and start banging away. Then I'll move on to the next one, have another coffee, and so on.

'But it's a discipline. I don't move around randomly. The night before I'll map out exactly where I want to get to in each cafe and stick to the plan. So if I've got, say, six sections to write I'll split each of them into three mini sections – so I can keep a track of my "lap times" within each one – and knock each of them out in a different location. It keeps both the mind, and the writing, fresh.

'Other times, if I'm zooming around on the bike, I'll schedule service station stops and do the same thing. Only problem is: coffee's not as good!'

Andy's rationale is spot on. Plan when and where you're going to accomplish a task and you're way more likely to get it done.

One study, for instance, looked at the ability of drug addicts to complete a simple assignment – not, as you might imagine, the most reliable of folk when it comes to seeing things through. The experiment couldn't have been easier. They had to write, and submit, a short essay. On time.

Sure enough, it turned out that those addicts who wrote down when and where they were going to put pen to paper were far more likely to come up with the goods.

So it's easy. If you want to be more productive:

- *draw up a task list,*
- *construct an itinerary, and*
- *get on your bike!*

Not literally, of course – unless you have a very understanding boss. But figuratively. From workstation to workstation. From the peaceful safe haven of an unused meeting room to a quiet corner on the far side of the lobby. Or, if you work from home, between different rooms in your house.

Remember:

- *keep your head down,*
- *don't talk to anyone, and*
- *don't let up 'til you get where you want to be.*

In other words, work clean.

'The key,' as Andy points out, 'is not to have time cut-offs between each location but to hit the road when you've finished the task you've set yourself. That way each task remains unique to each location and you maximize the novelty factor.'

## WHAT YOU DO
### Beware the morning after
## WHAT IT DOES

A simple one to finish off with. But important nonetheless. When Andy was talking just now about banging away in cafes (ahem, on his laptop) he mentioned something in passing: that he'd sketch out a plan of action the night before.

Now that may seem like basic common sense – and on the one hand, of course, it is. But on the other hand, it goes a bit deeper.

'Plan of Action' is basic common sense.

'Night before' is *science*.

The reason it's science is because of a study that was conducted several years ago on willpower. Or, rather, how much we overestimate it.

Results revealed that when we're in a so-called COLD state (in other words, *not* in the throes of temptation) we exhibit what's known as a *restraint bias*: we significantly miscalculate the amount of temptation we can *really* handle when the chips are down and we're in the grip of a HOT state.

Moreover, the study also showed that the greater your confidence in your capacity for self-control, the more likely you are to fold. Smokers, for example, who overegged their ability to kick the habit, were considerably more likely to whip out the fags after simply watching a film about smoking than their dubious, more ambivalent counterparts.

The moral of the story, as Andy points out, is threefold:

- *give your ego a smack in the mouth,*
- *err on the side of caution, and*
- *make things as easy as possible for yourself.*

'Sitting at home with a beer in one hand and the remote in the other, you may *think* that you'll be able to perch calmly at your desk and write out a to-do list in the morning,' he observes (COLD state). 'But when tomorrow rolls round [HOT state] it's a different ball game altogether. There's:

- *email to check*
- *your Facebook status to update*
- *Twitter to browse*
- *your ex to stalk*
- *that bloke who gave you his card at the conference last week to Google ...*

'Mental hygiene is paramount. Vices and weaknesses are like psychological bacteria. Under the right conditions they multiply ten to the dozen – when the structure isn't there and distraction gets its foot in the door. So it's extremely important that you keep your brain nice and clean.

'And when it comes to delivering, there's no better way than by starting the night before ... by cracking open a packet of fresh motivational Wet Wipes and committing to a plan of action.

'Constantly challenge yourself by asking yourself the same two questions over and over:

- What do I want to achieve by this time tomorrow?
- What do I have to say "no" to in order to make that happen?'

# 3. CONNECT

We've all played Snakes and Ladders. It's a simple game but it can take bloody hours. Up one minute, down the next … unless you just hit blanks all the way to a hundred.

'But where's the fun in that?' as Andy rightly asks.

Without the satisfaction of shooting up a ladder or the fiendish frustration of slithering down a snake, every square is the same: a monotonous procession of zero-gravity emotions glissading, as far as the die can see, towards some vaguely meaningless and arbitrarily inexorable terminus.

You can see why the game's such a good analogy for life!

I've always been fascinated by Snakes and Ladders, I tell Andy. Take a look at the sample board opposite. In a perfect game, you could reach 100 with just eight throws of the die:

- **FOUR SIXES to get you to 24**
- **A FOUR to bag the magic 28 ➜ 84**
- **TWO SIXES to hit 96, and then**
- **A FINAL FOUR to get you home and dry**

Has anyone ever done it? Who knows?
The fact is: it's *possible*!
Technically, with:

- **a good start**
- **one big break, and**
- **a bit of fancy footwork at the end …**

… you can be home and hosed before your opponent has

even got off the first rung of the board. The problem, needless to say, is that your fate is in the hands of the die.

Real life is full of snakes and ladders.

Get the wrong boss and you might, quite literally, find yourself back at square one at some company down the road. Or even switching careers.

Make the right contact at a conference, on the other hand, and you might find that your previously paltry portfolio quadruples in as many weeks.

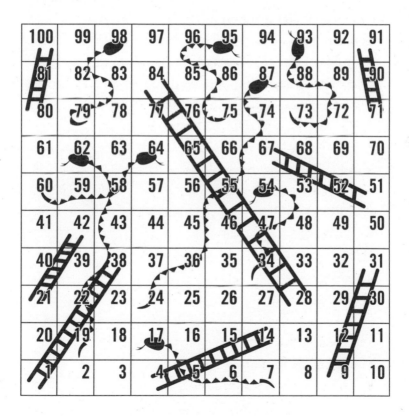

*0–100 in 8 throws*

'The difference in real life,' as Andy points out, 'is that, to a certain extent, you can influence how things turn out. Sure, some people might rely more on luck than judgement. And some people, just like in Snakes and Ladders, rely purely on luck.

'But:

- the right word in the right ear
- the right pitch to the right audience
- the right introduction at the right moment ...

'... can have you shinning up the rungs of success faster than a chimp with a banger stuck up its arse.'

The tricky part, of course, is identifying whose that ear, what that audience, and when that moment *is* exactly.

Andy: 'And then lighting the banger!'

# GOOD PSYCHOPATH TIPS

## Connect

Andy and I are having a sausage roll in one of Andy's office suites off the M6: Hilton Park Services. The Bard has got his email out.

'Here,' he says, 'have a gander at this. One of my old Regiment mates, Snapper, just sent it. Reminds me a bit of your Snakes and Ladders analogy … you know, right square and all that?'

He hands me the screen and I take a look.

Instantly, I feel my buttocks clench so tight they make Andy's wallet look like a laxative tester's rectum.

It's a *joke*. But this time, as it turns out, not a bad one.

*Father*: 'Son, I want you to marry a girl of my choice.'
*Son*: 'Thanks, Dad, but if it's all the same to you I think I'll choose my own bride.'
*Father*: 'But, son, the girl is Bill Gates's daughter.'
*Son*: 'Er, well, in that case … OK!'
Next, Father approaches Bill Gates.
*Father*: 'Bill, I reckon I've found a husband for your daughter.'
*Bill Gates*: 'But my daughter isn't interested in getting married!'
*Father*: 'But, Bill, this young man is a vice-president of the World Bank.'
*Bill Gates*: 'Er, well, in that case … OK!'
Finally, Father goes to see the president of the World Bank.
*Father*: 'Jim, I have a young man here I'd like to recommend

as a vice-president.'

*President*: 'Hey, that's great! But the problem is, I already have more vice-presidents than I need.'

*Father*: 'I know, I know. But you see, this young man is Bill Gates's son-in-law.'

*President*: 'Er, well, in that case ... OK!'

Ho ho! But you can see what we're getting at here. Life, the universe and everything ... it's all about personal relationships. In the cosmos, those relationships constitute the gravitational fields that exist between different forms of matter. In life it's the *psychological* fields that prevail:

- **between organizations,**
- **between the various sections that exist within those organizations, and**
- **between the individuals that comprise those sections.**

These social networks are invariably formed, and frequently enhanced, by encounters between individuals.

Business is no exception.

'You scratch my back and I won't stick a knife in yours!' as Andy rather courteously puts it, adding a whole new dimension to the concept of reciprocal altruism.

It's an open secret at many top firms, for instance, that the real interview process doesn't take place in the interview suite but over the dinner table afterwards and over drinks in the bar after that.

So next time you walk into a crowded room – be it at a conference, at a party or some other business gathering – remember that a carefully controlled introduction could save you six months' work. The following few tips will help you get the ball rolling. Or maybe that should be the die?

I'm afraid we can't promise that you won't hit a snake.

But you'll definitely go up in the world!

---

## WHAT YOU DO

**If you're invited – go!**

## WHAT IT DOES

---

Woody Allen once said that 80 per cent of success is showing up.

And science proves him right.

Research reveals that there's no such thing as a 'lucky' person – but that there *are* people who consistently 'get out more': who try their hand at lots of different things, who bend the ear of lots of different people … who put themselves, in other words, in positions where good things have a damn sight better chance of happening to them than if they simply spent the night, as the comedian Peter Cook once memorably put it, languishing on the couch catching up on their masturbation schedules. Take a look at the diagram on the next page.

In the quantum, quadratic universe of time and place, you've got a one-in-four chance of getting it right.

So given the fact that the Law of Averages is, more often than not, going to be against you, it makes perfect sense to maximize your chances of wasting your time in order to do the opposite: to maximize your chances of *not* wasting it!

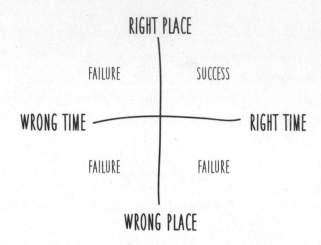

## TIME AND PLACE: ONE WITHOUT THE OTHER DOESN'T CUT IT

Andy gives a great example.

'The daughter of a friend of mine – well, actually, a friend of the missus – landed a job in a call centre some time back. It wasn't long before she was absolutely fucking sick of it and thinking of getting another one. Basically, what happened was this.

'On day one, the boss told her that the average hit rate was around one sale for every hundred calls – and *that*, right from the word go, is what did her in. From that moment on, every morning she got on the blower all she could think of was the shitload of rejections she was going to face that day.

'So much so that as time went on her call rate – and, of course, her hit rate – began to go down. But that, as I explained to her, is exactly what she *shouldn't* be doing. Rather than seeing those ninety-nine calls out of a hundred as being an *obstacle* to success, I told her, she should see them, instead, as being ninety-nine *stepping stones* to success. *Ninety-nine stepping stones to that one-percentage sale.*

'And if she thought of it in those terms then what she should be doing – if she wanted to impress the boss – is not shying away from making calls but precisely the opposite. Making way, way more calls than anyone else in the office. Rather than fearing those rejections she should welcome them with open arms, collect as many of them as she could.

'Because at the end of the day those were the tokens that eventually bought her the sale!

'Once she came round to seeing it like that, once she binned the self-esteem issues and began to toughen up, things started to change. In fact, a couple of months ago she was voted top salesperson of the quarter.'

## WHAT YOU DO
**Be yourself ...**

## WHAT IT DOES

... or, as Andy points out, not just yourself but your *best* self.

Think of the different skill sets that comprise your personality as being the players on a football team. *Your* football team. The one that *you* coach. The one that *you* put out every day.

If your natural formation is 4-4-2, then why play 4-5-1?

What manager wouldn't play to his team's strengths?

Likewise, if you have a star player on your team – let's say, a good listener – you need to make sure *they* have the run of the game and that other players – such as a nervous bullshitter, for instance – don't get under their feet. This, needless to say, requires a degree of self-knowledge and insight.

So to find out who you *really* are – to get a detailed breakdown of *your* personality profile – why not take the test at the end of this section? As Andy rightly observes: 'If you don't know the shape of your team, how can you call on your A game?'

## WHAT YOU DO
### Do your homework

## WHAT IT DOES

A man calls home and his five-year-old daughter picks up the phone.

'Hi, darling,' says the man. 'It's Daddy. Is Mummy around?'

'No, Daddy,' says the little girl. 'She's upstairs in the bedroom with Uncle Geoff.'

There's a brief pause.

'But, sweetie,' says the man, 'you don't have an Uncle Geoff.'

'I do,' says the little girl. 'And he's upstairs with Mummy in the bedroom.'

The man instantly becomes suspicious.

'OK, honey,' he says. 'Listen carefully to what I want you to do. I want you to put the phone down on the table, run upstairs to the bedroom, knock on the door, and tell Mummy that Daddy's car has just pulled into the driveway. Have you got that?'

'Yes,' says the little girl and scoots off.

A minute or so later she's back on the phone.

'Hi, Daddy,' she says, 'I've done what you asked me and Mummy and Uncle Geoff have gone crazy.'

The man can barely contain his anger.

'What do you mean, darling,' he asks, '"gone crazy"?'

'Well,' says the little girl, 'Mummy got very scared, jumped out of bed with no clothes on and ran around screaming. Then she tripped over the cat, banged her head on the floor, and now she's just lying there not moving.'

The man starts to panic.

'Oh my God! Call an ambulance quickly! What about your Uncle Geoff?'

The little girl starts to cry. 'Uncle Geoff was also scared and jumped out of bed with no clothes on,' she sobs. 'He dived out of the bedroom window into the swimming pool. But I guess he didn't know that you emptied out all the water last week to clean it. He's lying on the ground with blood pouring out of his head. I think he's dead.'

The man is speechless.

'Swimming pool?' he says. 'Hang on, what number is this?'

OK, OK, so this didn't actually happen.

Not that we know of anyway!

But be that as it may, it's a powerful, if rather extravagant demonstration of the paramount importance of gleaning basic, preliminary facts before launching into Spanish Inquisition mode.

'In the Regiment,' says Andy, 'in the CRW unit, we'd spend days studying the plans of buildings, working out the best points of access. It was all part of the training. You don't set a charge and blow in the windows if you can prise open a skylight and sneak in quietly.

'In a hostage rescue situation, your main weapon is surprise, and a heck of a lot of background research goes into making it a good one. It was exactly the same in Northern Ireland when we were targeting potential informants. We'd spend weeks looking into a person's background finding out their weak points so we could use them against them. And if, on the odd occasion, we drew a blank, there was always the good old gay-porn stash that suddenly appeared from nowhere. That usually did the trick!

'People are the same as buildings, Kev. There are good ways in and bad ways in. Back doors left unlocked and front desks full of security. It's up to you to find the one that works.'

Andy's 'access' analogy has a certain common-sense appeal to it – especially when it comes to social networking. Exactly like a hostage rescue situation, you often get just the one 'shot' at making an impression on a 'target' – and usually under considerable time pressure. So, just like Special Forces, it pays to put in the hours before you turn up in the black kit.

'You don't need to go overboard and start compiling Chilcot Reports on everyone,' says Andy. 'But doing a bit of behind-the-scenes detective work on the background and interests of the people you want to speak to not only gives you a massive head start when it comes to making small talk, it also gives you time to frame what you want to say to generate maximum appeal.'

Helpful here is the Elevator Pitch: a brief, persuasive speech lasting no more than 20–30 seconds – the duration of a short elevator journey – that you can prepare (and practise!) in advance to create interest in:

- *YOU*
- *Your PRODUCT*
- *Your PROJECT* …

… pretty much anything you want.

Here's what you need to know.

# THE ELEVATOR PITCH

What it is ...
- SHORT
- SHARP
- SUCCINCT

What it does ...
- Helps you go up in the world!

The golden rules ...
- ESTABLISH contact
- ENGAGE interest
- ENCOURAGE collaboration ...
  so throw in a statistic or two
  with the smile

## 1. Explain what you do

On the B of the Button Press, begin by outlining:

- **What PROBLEM you SOLVE**
- **What NEED you MEET**
- **What VALUE you PROVIDE**

Remember, no one wants to buy a drill. They want to buy a hole!

*Example: 'Hi, I develop mobile phone apps that organizations use to train their staff in their own time. This takes a significant chunk off the manager's workload.'*

## 2. Identify your USP (Unique Selling Proposition)

After you've established what you do, clarify what it is that you do that no one else does.

*Example: 'Unlike most other developers, our apps are tailor-made to suit individual requirements within individual organizations. Although this takes a bit more time – because we make a point of paying a dedicated visit to each business – it means that, on average, 95 per cent of our clients are satisfied with the first version of their app.'*

## 3. Invite feedback

This is best done in the form of a question that provides the other party with an opportunity to compare and contrast their own approach to the issue under discussion.

*Example: 'At the moment, how does your company go about training new people?'*

Putting it all together:

Hi, I develop mobile phone apps that organizations use to train their staff in their own time. This takes a significant chunk off the manager's workload.

Unlike most other developers, our apps are tailor-made to suit individual requirements within individual organizations. Although this takes a bit more time – because we make a point of paying a dedicated visit to each business – it means that, on average, 95 per cent of our clients are satisfied with the first version of their app.'

At the moment, how does your company go about training new people?

- *Deal done*
- *Doors open!*

---

## WHAT YOU DO
### Make it easy ...

## WHAT IT DOES
### ... for others to talk to you.

---

'Because,' as Andy points out, 'in situations like social gatherings where the script goes out the window and people feel a bit unsure of themselves, they're going to go for "easy" every time. This is why the ability to look the part is such a good trick to have up your sleeve. You often hear it said that *being* the part is the most important thing in life. But it doesn't always work like that. Often, if you don't look the part to begin with you'll never get the *chance* to be it!

'What people tend to forget when they attend social gatherings is that the movers and shakers are aware that they're being watched – and they certainly don't want to be seen talking to someone who other movers and shakers wouldn't want to be seen talking to! So it's simple. The first rule of thumb is to dress appropriately for the occasion. One of the things you learn in business after a while is that people dress in the way they want to be treated.

'If I turn up at a boardroom meeting and there's someone there, say, in ripped jeans, Converse trainers and a T-shirt – and it *has* been known! – I'll immediately think to myself: basically, this person wants to be treated like a seventeen-year-old. And what do seventeen-year-olds lack? Confidence.

'So what do they do? They try too hard. Don't fall into that trap – it's not a good look!

'If you want to be taken seriously by the big boys, then look as if you want to be taken seriously.

'On the other hand, that doesn't mean you've got to go around with a face like a slapped arse all day. I mean, who's going to want to talk to someone like that at a party? The first thing I'd think is that it might be someone from the Revenue!'

Once again, Andy's experience on the business coalface has *science* to back it up.

There are two different types of engine in our brains – the thinking (or cognitive) engine and the feeling (or emotional) one – and they run on two different kinds of gas. The cognitive engine, which in evolutionary terms is actually quite shiny and new, runs on reasoning and rational thought. It uses cold, hard logic to assess situations and weigh up alternatives.

The emotional engine, on the other hand – older, clunkier, fartier – is a bit more no-nonsense and runs on:

- *gut instincts,*
- *first impressions, and*
- *quick-and-dirty decision-making.*

This is the engine that powers what people think of us when they first meet us; the engine that tells us that looking the part is a good first step to being it.

Research, for instance, shows that if a stranger comes up to us in the street and asks for money to make a phone call, the more closely their appearance resembles ours, the more likely we are to give it to them.

It also shows that when someone smiles at us, it's virtually impossible for us not to smile back – increasing not just our own positive feelings but also the chances that any ensuing interaction will proceed smoothly. Smiling at the right time when negotiating, for example – such as at the beginning of the proceedings when the various protagonists are sizing each other up – not only elevates mood on both sides of the table but also produces:

- **more successful outcomes in business,**
- **higher sales ratios on the shop floor, and**
- **more lenient penalties in the courtroom! (Smiling evolved in our primate ancestors as an appeasement gesture to signify submission.)**

One study even looked at smugglers in airports and revealed that, contrary to what common sense might dictate, they smiled less on average than their innocent counterparts.

'Because smiling is rooted in submission, right?' offers Andy. 'So if you're honest and have nothing to hide then you're not going to have a problem with that. But if, on the other hand, you've got a couple of kilos of coke stashed in the heels of your Nikes, then your best bet's to signal threat. To dominate rather than appease. To deter a potential search before it even happens.'

Spot on.

Ever wondered why, when the police pull up next to you at the lights, you sit there grinning like an idiot at them? It's because even though everything's OK, their mere presence makes us feel guilty and we immediately go into appeasement mode.

'So next time,' says Andy, 'just to be on the safe side, give them the finger. Guaranteed they won't suspect a thing ...'

# 4. ENGAGE

'Back in the Eighties when I started working undercover in Northern Ireland,' Andy tells me, 'I remember talking to one of the intelligence lads who'd been handling enemy agents for years. He said that "turning" one of the players and getting them to work for you was a bit like cracking a safe: there was an influence code consisting of four different components and if, when you were dealing with your potential informant, you managed to get them all exactly right, then the door to their brain would miraculously spring open and you'd get them to do what you wanted.

'Now as you know, Kev, the army loves a good acronym, and this was no exception.' Because the four components he was talking about spelled out:

## SHIT!

- 'Be SURE in your own mind of what *you* want.
- 'HEAR what the *agent* is saying.
- 'INTEGRATE what you want them to do within a framework of communication that makes them feel comfortable. In other words:
    - minimize the fear factor,
    - gain their trust, and
    - make them "see sense".
- 'TUNE in to the player as an individual: find out what is important to them, then use it to your advantage.

'But you know what? It's funny. Over the years I've found that exactly the same approach works in business. In fact, it works in all walks of life … from the Bogside to the boardroom, you could say. Feed someone a load of SHIT and before you know it you'll have them eating out of the palm of your hand!'

# GOOD PSYCHOPATH TIPS

## Engage

Andy's acronym rang a few bells when he told it to me. It turned out that my own research into corporate negotiating styles had yielded something similar. Not only that but, as luck would have it, the four mirror-image components of successful business relationships that *I'd* uncovered comprised a nice little acronym of their own:

- *Familiarity*
- *Attentiveness*
- *Confidence, and*
- *Empathy*

## FACE!

… which, as you might notice, fits rather snugly with Andy's SHIT.

But alongside concerns over academic rigour, there's also the need for scientific decorum … and so, in the interests of intellectual good taste, putting the two acronyms together probably *isn't* a good idea. Let's for the moment then just concentrate on FACE and briefly examine each of the components in turn to see how they contribute to positive, constructive and profitable interactions.

---

## WHAT YOU DO

**Close-quarter conversations**
**STRATEGY 1: FAMILIARITY**

## WHAT IT DOES

In a study conducted several years ago, researchers found that secretly morphing the faces of voters with political candidates significantly increased the probability that those voters would endorse those candidates – even though they had no idea that the politicians' faces comprised appreciable elements of their own.

Take a look at the mugshot below, for instance: 50 per cent Andy and 50 per cent ME!

*Andy McDutton*

If Andy was running for office (and let's hope for all our sakes that never happens), then I'd be way more likely to vote for him on the evidence of this photo than if the image was 100 per cent McNab. And vice-versa.

The reason? Because our brains, even though we're not aware of it most of the time, have a hardwired preference for the things we find familiar.

Now in everyday conversation, of course, we can't start mutating into other people whenever we feel like it. But we *can* create the impression of familiarity in other ways. Subtly mirroring the body language and speech patterns (especially the rate and intonation of speech) of the person you're talking to, for instance, dramatically increases rapport.

As does:

- touch (on the arm, just above the elbow, no more than twice during a ten-minute encounter)
- the use of first names (once at the beginning and once at the end of a conversation)
- the conspiratorial lean-in (a single, shared, under-the-counter 'confidence' delivered directly into the ear* of the other person), and
- self-disclosure (the social psychological principle of reciprocity dictates that if you want someone to tell you something about *them*selves you first have to tell them something about *your*self)

But a word of caution. All of these things need to be done circumspectly and in moderation. After all, as Andy points out: 'If someone kept touching *my* arm, whispering sweet nothings in *my*

---

*Research has shown that if you want to be more persuasive you should position yourself to the left of the person you wish to influence, getting them to orient their head towards you as you speak into their left ear, thereby engaging the right hemisphere of their brain. Precisely why this might be is unclear. One theory is that the superior language ability of the brain's left hemisphere renders it more adept at counter-arguing than the right. Another suggests that the language system of the left hemisphere is intrinsically linked with a cognitive system that strives for order and consistency, therefore making it more resistant to attitude change. Andy's take on it is somewhat more pragmatic: 'As long as it works … who cares?'

ear, copying what *I* did, and didn't shut up, they'd just get a fucking slap, mate!

'Unless they were Sienna Miller ...'

## WHAT YOU DO
### Close-quarter conversations
### STRATEGY 2: ATTENTIVENESS

## WHAT IT DOES

Not rocket science, this one.

We've all been lumbered with someone at a party who hogs the conversation and can't keep their trap shut. What do we do? We walk away, that's what.

So why do it yourself? Psychological impressions of people with verbal diarrhoea consistently tag them as one of three Ns. They're nervous, narcissistic or nuts.

At the end of the day, it usually makes no difference because whichever one it is, you don't really want to do business with them, do you? Add to this the other side of the coin – that, afforded both the platform and the encouragement, most people generally find it very hard to resist the opportunity to talk about themselves – and it is, as Andy says, a no-brainer.

'Going up to someone at a function and introducing yourself is like drawing up a social contract. It's as much an invitation for that person to tell you about *them*selves as it is an opportunity for *you* to tell them about *your*self,' he observes. 'It is not, as many people think, a mandate for *you* to bombard them with facts about *your*self and not let them get a word in edgeways. Now, if the other person is skilled they'll hand you the floor at some point anyway.

You've just got to bide your time ... and remember that people are way more likely to listen to *you* if you start by listening to *them*.'

When it comes down to it, it's basic common sense. But it's not just in social situations that the ability to shut up and listen pays dividends. It works across the board. Good listeners* have been shown to:

- Generate better figures on the sales floor
- Attain more successful outcomes around the negotiating table
- Achieve higher performance ratings in positions of power
- As managers, provide greater job satisfaction
- As doctors, provide better care for their patients

'*Silent* and *listen* contain the same six letters,' observes Andy. 'Funny that!'

```
-------------------------- WHAT YOU DO ---------------------------
                     Close-quarter conversations
                      STRATEGY 3: CONFIDENCE
-------------------------- WHAT IT DOES --------------------------
```

Of all the high-end, off-the-peg personality characteristics you see displayed in the windows of psychology's upmarket, designer-label boutiques, confidence is the one that keeps the fakers and counterfeiters in business. That's because, to the untrained eye,

---

*We shall be looking at the art of listening in more detail later in the social intelligence section.

fake confidence is pretty much indistinguishable from the real thing. Only the person wearing it knows the difference.

Of course, as Andy points out, *real* self-assurance *does* have its advantages. 'The genuine article is built to last,' he rightly observes, 'and doesn't fall apart in the wash.'

But if you're still saving up for that authentic ring of confidence and want to appear slick and sassy, then the bootleg variety certainly won't do you any harm.

Investing in confidence is definitely worth the effort. Why? Because although most of us like to *think* that we evaluate others primarily on the basis of talent and smarts and ability, we frequently do precisely the opposite – sometimes with damaging consequences:

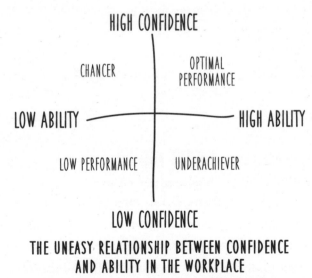

**THE UNEASY RELATIONSHIP BETWEEN CONFIDENCE AND ABILITY IN THE WORKPLACE**

Time pressure necessitates that we cut psychological corners and give undue weight to superficial accoutrements of competence: confidence being chief among them. Case in point: a recent survey of students, academics and others in the workplace showed that those who appeared more confident in their abilities – irrespective of whether or not they really *were* any better than their peers – not only achieved positions of higher social status but also tended to:

- be more admired,
- more listened to, and
- exert greater influence over the group when it came to making decisions.

In a general knowledge quiz, for example, those who proffered the loudest, proudest and most ostentatious answers were held in the highest regard – even when those answers were wrong.

So if we rule out being lairy, then – remember the importance of letting others do the talking – how else might confidence translate into social performance?

'Well,' says Andy, 'there are a number of ways. First, it can be in the way you approach people. Never hesitate! As soon as you make eye contact with someone or enter their personal space: smile, say hello, open with your leading question, and then shut up and listen to what they have to say.'

Absolutely right!

Here's an interesting fact for anyone going out on the pull in the near future. From the moment the person you are looking at notices you checking them out, you've got three seconds to get across there and say something. That's right. Just three!

After that your creep-out credentials begin rising with every eye-blink.

'Secondly,' says Andy, 'if you're attending a function, forget all that "fashionably late" bollocks. Because it really *is* bollocks. Get where you're going on time, or at worst within fifteen minutes of the event starting, because if you leave it any later conversational cliques will already have formed and you'll look like Billy No Mates. Rather than appearing cool, hip and trendy, you'll look awkward and uncomfortable – not a good confidence-builder or -inspirer.

'Thirdly, resist the temptation to rush into a room and jump straight in with your pals. That's just your nerves getting the better of you. For starters, you can chat to them any time. But there's also something else. One of the little tricks you learn when you're working undercover is that anyone who's anyone keeps their eyes on one thing: the entrance to the room. And what's true in the drugs and guns world is also the same in business. So instead:

- **Walk in slowly.**
- **Step to the right of the door.**
- **Pause for twenty to thirty seconds (if you want you can use that time – in 'theatre', as it were – to go quickly through your mission statement).**
- **Smile, and then**
- **Make your entrance proper.**

'That way you'll have dipped your toe in the room and got a feel for the social temperature *plus* you'll have allowed those of importance who are already there to notice you and clock your arrival.

'Finally, don't settle down and take up permanent residency with any one group or individual. Not only will you outstay your visa, but people will think you're clingy and a drain on resources. Instead, make it a round-the-room trip and get as many stamps as you can on your agenda passport.

'How long should you spend in each conversation before you

get the ferry to the next one? There's no set answer to that question. It all depends on how things are going at the time. As a general principle I use my old cup-of-tea rule. Imagine that, from the moment you introduce yourself to someone, you stick the kettle on. The aim of the exercise is to be sitting down having a brew in five or so minutes thinking about what you've got out of them.'

Hmm ... tea. I stroke my chin. Really, Andy?

He smiles. 'And that's another thing,' he says. 'Booze is for wimps. Real men drink Shirley Temples!'

---

## WHAT YOU DO
### Close-quarter conversations
### STRATEGY 4: EMPATHY

## WHAT IT DOES

Andy and I are in the middle of doing a signing in a small indie bookstore up north. He comes up to me during the break:

> I went into *my* local bookshop the other day and the assistant there was bored out of her mind.
>> 'Hey,' I said, 'I'm looking for a book on lack of empathy.'
>> She just looks at me and shrugs.
>> 'Do I look like I give a fuck?' she says.
>> 'Yeah,' I go, 'that's the one!'

Another side-splitter from Mr Frigging Hilarious.

But actually, as he well knows, Andy's joke captures a common misconception about empathy that most people share. Contrary to popular belief, empathy is *not* about showing concern for other people. That's sympathy. Instead, empathy is about being able to put yourself in someone else's shoes, to see things as they see them.

There's a subtle difference. Think about it. On the one hand, I can quite easily feel concern for a dolphin caught up in a shark net without actually knowing what it's like. On the other hand, I'm also perfectly capable of imagining what it's like to be a fan of the losing side in the FA Cup final.

But, hey, if my side's lifting the silverware, do you think I give a toss?

So just to clarify then, it's *empathy* we're talking about here, not sympathy – and in business interactions it's an invaluable commodity to bring to any table.

Andy gives a simple example.

'An old mate of mine in the Regiment started up as a security consultant when he left,' he tells me. 'Anyway, as you do, he went and got these business cards done. You should've seen them. For a start, they were made of metal. But that wasn't all. One edge was smooth and had "coke" inscribed on it while the other one was serrated and had "windpipe". Genius!

'I mean, who's going to throw one of those away? You're going to do the opposite, aren't you? You're going to keep it on you and get it out of your wallet to show other people. Which is exactly what happened. Within six months of starting he was one of the best known lads on the circuit.'

In the corporate arena then, this is what empathy is all about: working out what makes others tick and second-guessing what they're going to do. Nine times out of ten the answer is simple:

- **What's in it for *me*?**
- **What am *I* going to get out of it?**

Ever wondered how long mortgages have been about?

The answer is since Biblical times. According to the American Law Register of 1865, it seems that the Ancient Israelites first came up with the idea and that it then caught on in Greek and Roman culture.

Now banks don't lend you money to buy a house out of goodwill, do they? They do so because of one word: INTEREST. Odd, don't you think, that they decided to call it that? Of course, 'interests' vary from person to person and from time to time … which means that it's important to do your homework (more on that in a bit) before you ask anyone for anything.

Case in point: I once remember watching two kids arguing over the last can of Coke in a shop. In the end Mum pulled both of them away and they ended up with nothing. Later, during the post-mortem on the bus, it turned out that one of them had wanted it because he was thirsty and the other one had wanted it because he was collecting the tokens on the back.

A little prior research … and everyone's a winner!

Andy comes up with an example from the time he was on the board of a certain FTSE 250 telecommunications company.

'One of the guys had an idea for a big in-house computer software conference,' he tells me. 'It was one of those classic cases where everyone loved it but no one wanted to put up the money. Eventually he got so obsessed with it that they gave him the nickname 999 megs – because he couldn't quite nail the gig! Then one night, at some glitzy corporate love-fest forty floors up in Manhattan, he runs into the editor of one of the world's top geek magazines. *Aha*, he thinks. "What if I frame the conference not as a conference but as an expo … as a unique, market-leading trade fair? Not only would that be something this guy would want on his front cover, it would be something this guy would *pay a lot of money for* to have on his front cover!" Guess whose face was all over the newsstand in WH Smith six months later …'

# 5. LIMIT THE VARIABLES

Familiar with this kind of scenario?

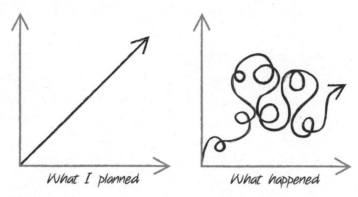

What I planned      What happened

As John Lennon once said: 'Life is what happens when you're busy making other plans.'

The former double Olympic Gold-medallist turned Tory MP turned athletics impresario Sebastian Coe certainly is. In his autobiography *Running My Life*, Lord Coe tells the story of how, in 1997, as personal assistant to the then Leader of the Opposition William Hague, he was tasked with overseeing a visit by his charge to the Lancastrian seaport of Fleetwood, a once-prosperous fishing community just north of Blackpool.

The visit was to take place during the annual party conference – Hague's first as Tory leader – and so was bound to attract media attention.

A week before the excursion was due to take place, Coe began mustering his enviable reserves of organizational acumen and set about planning the trip in meticulous detail.

He went up to Fleetwood for a recce, chewed the fat with the skippers of several trawlers and listened to their concerns – as ominous as they were inevitable – over the substantial challenges faced by the community in the light of a fragile offshore ecology: the vexed question of catch quotas and declining fish stocks being the primary bone of contention. The discussions went well and the charm offensive, seemingly, had worked.

So much so that, come the day of the visit, Coe was quietly confident that – to quote his father's performance-enhancing mantra during his previous career on the track – he'd 'limited the variables' as much as was humanly possible and that the Conservative leader's stopover would make for a favourable story.

After all, what was there not to like? It was a serious issue on the one hand but packed with human interest on the other. The photo opportunities would be huge.

As it turned out, they *were*, but not in the way that Coe had initially envisaged.

On arrival at the quayside it immediately transpired that the sea was out of the office, and would remain that way for the next few hours – locked, as it was, in an important meeting several miles offshore. As if that wasn't bad enough, a storm the previous night had prevented most of the vessels from returning – and those that remained were a sorry sight indeed: stuck, ingloriously, in the Morecambe Bay mud and clearly not going anywhere.

In the pantheon of metaphors it was less a car crash and more a shipwreck of a story. In fact, were one to have been trawling for such bounty – as, of course, the waiting media *were* – the pickings were rich and plentiful; ramshackle, clapped-out craft haplessly beached in the mire of an outmoded economy … and the leader of Her Majesty's opposition marooned on the quayside right there in front of them gaping gormlessly out to sea at an angry, foreboding horizon.

For Coe, it was a salutary lesson – and one that he never forgot.

He'd been *so* intent on limiting his old man's variables, so completely transfixed on ensuring his protégé stayed out of hot water, that he'd neglected to control the most important variable of all … whether or not there'd be any water to start with.

Andy and I are sitting in a cafe along the Bethnal Green Road in London's East End. Outside, some Barbour-jacketed idiot in a canary yellow Hyundai is making an absolute Horlicks of a U-ey.

Andy takes a sip of his Typhoo. No posh coffee round here.

'Look at that dipstick,' he says. 'I've known milk turn quicker.'

We laugh.

'You know,' I say, '*my* old man was pretty good at limiting the variables. I'll give you an example. I've never been much cop at reversing round corners. And years ago when I was learning to drive I was even worse. Anyway, coming up to my driving test I was convinced I was going to fail. "Look, Dad," I said, "I've got about as much chance of passing this test as George Best has of passing an off-licence. I can do all the other stuff. But as soon as they ask me to reverse round a corner I'm fucked. I might as well just run someone over."

'My old man just smiles. "You'll be fine, Kev," he says. "Trust me." Now, I'd never trusted my old man, Andy. He made Del Boy look like the Dalai Lama. But on this occasion I had no choice. If I cancelled the test at this stage I'd just lose my money. So, who dares wins, right? Anyway, the big day finally rolls round …

> … and I make my way to the test centre. The examiner checks my eyesight. No problem. We get on our way and I'm driving great. Emergency stop? Nail it! Three-point turn? Piece of piss! Eventually, towards the end of the test, the dreaded moment

comes. 'Right,' says the examiner, 'about 400 metres up on the left I want you to pull over when I tell you and reverse round the corner to the rear. OK?'

'OK,' I say. The next thirty seconds feels like an hour. All of a sudden I'm sweating like a glassblower's arse. But then, completely out of the blue, the examiner changes his mind. 'Bloody hell! Just keep going, will you,' he says. 'Look at that. Some prat has stopped right on the corner. I'm afraid we're just going to have to give you the benefit of the doubt, Mr Dutton. What a pillock! Take a left at the crossroads and we'll head back to the test centre.'

Well, as you can imagine I hardly needed telling twice. 'Sure,' I say, and start indicating left. And then, as the corner of doom approaches, I can hardly believe my eyes. There, parked right slap bang in the middle of the intersection, is my old man's dilapidated Datsun. Battered, brown and brakeless, I'd recognize that thing anywhere. It was like a turd on wheels. And behind it, as I chug past, there's my old man … cigar in hand, broad grin on his face, thumb raised aloft!

PASS!

Back at the flat an hour or so later there's a bottle of Moët on the table.

'How the fuck did you know?' I ask, as Dad grabs some glasses. 'I mean … that it was going to be that corner?'

He picks up the bottle and pops the cork.

'Easy,' he says. 'Last couple of weeks I've been following some of the tests around. And it's always the same one – right at the end, by Mrs Harris's. See, son, it's like I've always told you. If you want to get on in life it doesn't just pay to know what's *round* the corner. It also pays to know what's *on it*!'

# PERSONALITY QUESTIONNAIRE

Indicate the extent to which you agree or disagree with each of the statements by putting a cross in the appropriate space. There are no 'right' or 'wrong' answers to these statements – they measure individual behavioural preferences, not the presence of a 'good' or 'bad' personality. When you have finished, have a read over the scoring instructions below to see how you got on.

| | | Disagree strongly | Disagree moderately | Neither agree nor disagree | Agree moderately | Agree strongly |
|---|---|---|---|---|---|---|
| 1 | I work systematically. | ○ | ○ | ○ | ○ | ○ |
| 2 | I am a rather reserved person. | ○ | ○ | ○ | ○ | ○ |
| 3 | I worry about a lot of things. | ○ | ○ | ○ | ○ | ○ |
| 4 | I find it easy to forgive others. | ○ | ○ | ○ | ○ | ○ |
| 5 | I am a creative person. | ○ | ○ | ○ | ○ | ○ |
| 6 | I care about others a lot. | ○ | ○ | ○ | ○ | ○ |
| 7 | It is important for me to be organized. | ○ | ○ | ○ | ○ | ○ |
| 8 | I don't pay much attention to details. | ○ | ○ | ○ | ○ | ○ |
| 9 | I like starting conversations with people I don't know. | ○ | ○ | ○ | ○ | ○ |
| 10 | I have a poor imagination. | ○ | ○ | ○ | ○ | ○ |
| 11 | I am an efficient worker. | ○ | ○ | ○ | ○ | ○ |
| 12 | It doesn't take much for me to feel blue. | ○ | ○ | ○ | ○ | ○ |
| 13 | I can be rude sometimes. | ○ | ○ | ○ | ○ | ○ |
| 14 | I am usually relaxed. | ○ | ○ | ○ | ○ | ○ |
| 15 | I am a warm person. | ○ | ○ | ○ | ○ | ○ |
| 16 | I feel comfortable with being the centre of attention. | ○ | ○ | ○ | ○ | ○ |
| 17 | I am interested in many different things. | ○ | ○ | ○ | ○ | ○ |
| 18 | My mood changes frequently. | ○ | ○ | ○ | ○ | ○ |
| 19 | I am sociable and outgoing. | ○ | ○ | ○ | ○ | ○ |
| 20 | I like to think about abstract ideas. | ○ | ○ | ○ | ○ | ○ |

## SCORING INSTRUCTIONS

This simple personality questionnaire is designed to evaluate the five main character dimensions (the so-called 'Big Five') that research has shown makes up each of our personalities.

There are twenty items in the questionnaire: four for each of the aforementioned Big Five scales:

- *Neuroticism (N)*
- *Extraversion (E)*
- *Openness to Experience (O)*
- *Agreeableness (A)*
- *Conscientiousness (C)*

So ... how did you get on?

Well, first let's work out your score for **N**.

These are items: 3, 12, 14 and 18.

One of these items is *reverse scored*: item 14. Mark an 'R' next to that item on the grid.

Now, for the NON-REVERSE SCORED items allocate yourself the following points:

- *Disagree Strongly = 0*
- *Disagree Moderately = 1*
- *Neither Agree Nor Disagree = 2*
- *Agree Moderately = 3*
- *Agree Strongly = 4*

And use this scale for the REVERSE-SCORED item:

- *Disagree Strongly = 4*
- *Disagree Moderately = 3*
- *Neither Agree Nor Disagree = 2*
- *Agree Moderately = 1*
- *Agree Strongly = 0*

The sum of the four items represents your total score for N (Neuroticism).

Next, do the same thing to work out your scores for E, O, A and C. The following are the items corresponding to each scale, with the reverse-scored ones marked in **bold**:

- *E (Extraversion): **2**, 9, 16, 19*
- *O (Openness to experience): 5, **10**, 17, 20*
- *A (Agreeableness): 4, 6, **13**, 15*
- *C (Conscientiousness): 1, 7, **8**, 11*

When you have calculated your points totals for each of the five dimensions, check them against the scoring key below:

**0–3**    Very Low
**4–6**    Low
**7–11**   Average
**12–14**  High
**15–16**  Very High

# WHAT YOUR SCORES SAY ABOUT YOU

## Neuroticism

**LOW** You are calm, relaxed, stable and emotionally resilient … even under pressure.

**AVERAGE** You are generally relaxed and stress-resistant but sometimes experience negative emotions.

**HIGH** You are tense, anxious, highly strung and insecure … at the best of times!

## Extraversion

**LOW** You are reserved, shy and self-contained … you prefer your own company or that of a few close friends.

**AVERAGE** You are moderately outgoing and appreciate both time alone and social activities.

**HIGH** You are fun-loving, outgoing and gregarious … you love social situations.

## Openness to Experience

**LOW** You are practical, conformist and conventional … you have a narrow range of interests and like routine.

**AVERAGE** You tend to favour a balance between old and new ways.

**HIGH** You are imaginative, curious, creative … you like adventure and trying out new things.

## Agreeableness

**LOW** You are hard-nosed, competitive and abrasive … you don't mind ruffling a few feathers.

**AVERAGE** You are generally kind and affable but at times can be sceptical and uncompromising.

**HIGH** You are good-natured, helpful and soft-hearted … you are warm and empathic and tuned in to the feelings of others.

## Conscientiousness

**LOW** You are carefree, impulsive, disorganized and sometimes negligent … attention to detail is not one of your strong points!

**AVERAGE** There is some degree of method in your madness! You generally work to achieve your goals but also maintain a good work–life balance.

**HIGH** You are careful, fastidious, dependable and highly self-disciplined … you have high standards and a strong work ethic.

*AUTHORS' NOTE:*

*This simple personality questionnaire measures differences among normal individuals. It is not psychometrically validated nor is it a test of intelligence or ability, or a means of diagnosing problems of mental health or adjustment. It does, however, give you some idea about what makes you unique in your ways of thinking, feeling and interacting with others.*

 THREE

# HOW TO BE MORE SOCIALLY INTELLIGENT

'You know, my wife says my people skills
are like my cooking skills.
Quick and tasteless.'

Lt. Col. Nicholas Kudrow (*Mercury Rising*)

Early one morning the colonel's sitting in his office having a cup of tea when the phone rings.

It's bad news.

Private Jones's mother has died.

He calls in the sergeant and tells him.

'You'd better inform Jones asap,' he says.

The sergeant nods.

Ten minutes later the troops are all lined up ready for inspection on the parade ground.

'Right, listen in, men!' barks the sergeant. 'Brown, I want you to report to the front office for cleaning duties. Smith, I want you to go and see the quartermaster to sign out some new equipment. The rest of you ... get into your PT kit and I'll see you outside the gym in fifteen. Oh, and by the way, Jones, your mother died. Go and see the colonel!'

Jones does as he's told and the colonel offers his condolences and gives him seventy-two hours' compassionate leave.

Later that day the colonel runs into the sergeant in the mess hall.

'Sergeant,' he says, 'that was a pretty callous way to tell Jones that his mother had just died. Next time, er ... maybe exercise a bit more tact?'

'Of course, sir,' replies the sergeant.

A few months later the colonel gets another phone call.

Private Collins's mother has died.

He calls in the sergeant.

'Sergeant,' he says, 'I've just received word that Private Collins's mother passed away in the night. Would you be so good as to give him the sad news and to tell him to come in and see me?

'Oh ... and, sergeant, remember what I said to you the last time? This time be a bit more circumspect?'

'Yes, sir!' replies the sergeant.

Ten minutes later, the troops are out on the parade ground.

'OK, men,' yells the sergeant. 'Everyone whose mother is still alive and kicking take two steps forward. Er, Collins ... where do you think you're going?'

All of us know someone like this.

People with about as much discretion as a gorilla on speed.

What they're lacking is something called social intelligence. In short, people smarts – an essential companion to optimally functional interaction in the social domain. In simple terms, social intelligence refers to the cognitive and emotional know-how required to detect and decode a kaleidoscope of verbal and non-verbal cues ... and to successfully navigate the choppy evolutionary trade routes of modern-day social seas without getting beached or shipwrecked.

'What, you mean like that palm reader we saw in Skegness the other week?' Andy pipes up. '*She* was good at detecting and decoding stuff. "You are lonely, single and haven't had a partner for some time," she went. "I can tell from the blisters!"'

'Er, kind of,' I say, trying not to laugh. 'She did exude a certain insightfulness. But I was actually thinking of people who are a bit more – I dunno – *integrated* into society? You know, your spies, politicians, diplomats … People who aren't just good at picking up on stuff but are equally good at moving it around and putting it back down in a better place than they found it.'

You certainly know one when you see one. Unlike general intelligence, which is predominantly genetic, social intelligence is largely a product of our environment. We learn it. It develops through experience. And, as with most things in life, there are always going to be some jammy bastards further up the smarts ladder than others.

As a rule of thumb people high in social intelligence tend to fit the following profile. They are:

### Great social expressionists

- They possess exceptional verbal fluency.
- They're able to converse on a vast number of topics with a wide variety of people.
- They're able to think on their feet and calibrate both the tone and content of their communication to the particular dynamic of the discussion or conversation they happen to be in at the time … making them adept at both avoiding and resolving conflict.

### Consummate character actors

- They know how to play the game of social interaction and are able to effortlessly slip in and out of appropriate roles and personas during social encounters, giving them an air of supreme self-confidence.

### Skilled listeners

- They're experts at rapport-building.

### Accomplished people watchers

- They're brilliant at tuning in to what others are saying or doing, and reading what they're *really* thinking.

### Gifted persuaders

- They're masters of the art of framing what they want in such a way as to make it seem positively unreasonable not to let them have it!

Of course, it goes without saying that some of us are going to excel in some domains of social intelligence but not others: in the same way, for instance – when it comes to general intelligence – that some of us might have good spatial ability but fall down on verbal reasoning.

But if you want to get along with people – a tried-and-tested strategy of enhanced wellbeing! – then it certainly doesn't do any harm to brush up on the basics.

Here are a few to get you started …

## STOP HEARING, START LISTENING

The late Tommy Cooper used to tell a joke.

> One morning I knocked at my friend's door and his wife answered. I said, 'Is Jim in?' She didn't reply, just stood there looking at me. So I asked her again: 'Is Jim in?'
>
> Just then a woman appeared by her side. 'Sorry, luv,' she said. 'We buried him last Thursday.'
>
> 'Oh,' I said. 'He didn't happen to mention anything about a pot of paint before he went, did he?'

This gag usually raises a smile (especially the way Cooper used to tell it). But, as Andy points out, it's not exactly *funny*, is it? More … odd. Surreal. Crass, even.

The point, of course, is this: it's difficult to believe someone could be so insensitive. Could lack so much care and compassion. It's just too far removed from normal life, from basic human decency. That's the interpretation most people come up with, anyway. But maybe the truth is more straightforward. Maybe, in the joke as in everyday life, Cooper did have care and compassion. Lots of it, in fact. Maybe at the end of the day he just hadn't listened.

Listening is to hearing what seeing is to looking. Check this out:

I got a dig bick.
You that read wrong.
You read that wrong too.

Shocking, isn't it?

Not the message. Which, after all, makes no sense. ('You're telling me!' interjects Andy.) But the fact that we can get it so wrong. The reason, as you've probably guessed, is all down to one simple thing: 'Our brain's persistent and hard-wired preoccupation with bunking off school,' as Andy puts it.

When we look at a word, we tend to swallow it whole instead of chomping on its constituent components. As a result, as long as the first and last letters remain the same, our unrefined cognitive palates are more than happy to wolf it down in one as opposed to chewing it over.

Well, guess what?

It's the same when we hear someone talking. Most of the time, as long as we see their lips moving in sync and detect words coming out of their mouths, we're perfectly happy to just shunt our brains on to autopilot and let whatever they happen to be saying go in one ear and out the other.

'Which is why,' as Andy observes, 'things so often go tits up. Do it often enough, for long enough, and on enough occasions when you shouldn't, and you're going to wind up in the shit. No two ways about it.

'You're going to end up:

- *scammed*
- *screwed*
- *stuffed*
- *shafted, and probably*
- *single!*

'Probably all at the same time if you really go for it!'

# GOOD PSYCHOPATH TIPS

## Develop Listening Skills

You know, it's funny. To be a good listener, care and compassion are not, as many people might think, prerequisites. Among the best listeners I've ever met are some of the world's top conmen.

Here's one of them – a Kentucky-fried psychopath from America's Deep South, who had the coldest, clearest electric blue eyes imaginable and the coolest, sharpest, most exquisitely tailored wardrobe this side of Milan:

> One of the most important things a grifter must have in his possession is a good vulnerability radar. Most folk you come across pay no attention to what they say when they're talking to you. Once out, the words are gone.
>
> But a grifter will zone in on everything … Like therapy, you're trying to get inside the person. Figure out who they are from the little things. And it's always the little things. The devil's in the detail … You get them to open up, usually by telling them something about yourself first – a good grifter always has a narrative. And then immediately change the subject. Randomly. Abruptly. It can be anything … Some thought that just occurred to you out of the blue or whatever … anything to interrupt the flow of conversation.
>
> Nine times out of ten the person will completely forget what they've just said. Then you can get to work – not right

away, you need to be patient. But a month or two later. You modify whatever it is, whatever the hell they've told you – you tend to know instantly where the pressure points are – and then tell the story back as if it were your own.

BAM! From that point on, you can pretty much take what you want.

I'll give you an example ... [one guy is] rich, successful, works like a dog ... when he's a kid, he comes home from school to find his record collection gone. His pop's a bum and has sold it to stock up his liquor cabinet. The kid's been collecting these records for years.

So, wait, I think. You're telling me this after, what, three or four hours in a bar? There's something going down.

Then I get it. So *that's* why you work so goddamned hard, I think. It's because of your pappy. You're scared. Your life's been on hold all these years. You're not a CEO, you're that scared little kid. The one who's going to come home from school one day and find your record collection is history.

Jesus! I think. That's hilarious!

So guess what? A couple of weeks later I tell him what happened to *me*. How I get home from work one night and find my wife in bed with the boss. How *she* files for divorce. And cleans *me* out. Total bullshit! But you know what? I did that guy a favour. Put him out of his misery. What do they say – the best way to overcome your fears is to confront them?

Well, someone had to be Daddy.


By an odd coincidence, Andy and I were in the Record and Tape Exchange in London's Notting Hill when I first told him this story – trying to track down some limited-edition Clash album he'd had on purple vinyl back in the 1980s.

'Sounds like if that guy's life had taken a different turn he could've been a top negotiator,' he said, a battered old copy of *London Calling* in his hand. 'The blokes I used to work with in the Regiment – in fact, the blokes I work with *now* in the City – are all like him. Cold as ice. When they're negotiating with someone, they don't have any feelings for them – although they're good at faking it. No, instead they're like predators – totally zoned into the minutiae of the conversation and constantly on the look-out for:

- *weak spots*
- *inconsistencies, and*
- *areas of common ground* …

'… that they can capitalize on and exploit. Which all makes perfect sense given the nature of the game they're in. When the shit hits the fan, these are the guys who do the psychological abseiling, who take up position on the mental rooftops and balconies trying to get a clear line of fire.

'Any feelings about the people they have in their crosshairs – either positive or negative – can severely compromise their judgement and get in the way of the job. It might prevent them from pulling the trigger when they should, or spur them into pulling it when they shouldn't.'

Andy's absolutely right.

Every top negotiator I've ever met – be it in the military or the corporate arena – has been a master exponent of *listening through the crosshairs*. They may well be light on feelings, these psychological assassins, these shadowy emotional serial killers, but each and every one of them is custodian of an ancient secret – a core foundational secret – of black-belt influence:

If you want to be listened to, you must first learn to listen yourself.

Here's how they do it – and how you can do it, too.

---

## WHAT YOU DO
### Button it!

## WHAT IT DOES

---

'Without exception,' Andy observes, 'every hostage negotiator and corporate mediator I've ever worked with has one ability above all others: the ability to make whoever they happen to be talking to at the time feel like the most important person on earth. And do you know how they do it? By shutting up! They allow the other person to talk without interruption. The golden rule of being a good listener is to listen. The "good" bit comes later.'

Andy's point might be an obvious one but it's so often overlooked.

Few of us are going to be chewing the fat with ISIL commanders any time soon, so let's switch our focus to listening in everyday life. Cast your mind back to the last time you had a disagreement with your partner, a friend or a work colleague. How long did you let them speak before deciding to weigh in with a few 'home truths' of your own? Exactly!

That's not listening.

That's trying to win the argument – a completely different ballgame.

So next time you find yourself in a similar situation (won't be long!), get off the stage, as Andy puts it, and give the other person the floor. Pull up a pew in the dress circle and study their performance in silence. You'll be amazed at what you pick up – and how grateful they are for the chance to grab the limelight.

---

# WHAT YOU DO
### It's not about *you*, it's about *them*
# WHAT IT DOES

Any half-decent spotlight demands elevated levels of localized, low-lying narcissism in anyone who dares to step into it … which is why experienced negotiators and mediators are rarely seen anywhere near them, preferring instead to observe from the sanctuary of the stalls.

This canny juxtaposition of being close to the performance on the one hand but not actually part of it on the other permits them the luxury of not having to worry about putting on a show of their own and enables them instead to focus solely on the one in front of them.

In everyday life, as Andy points out, such detachment can be a game changer. 'Think about all the classic things we do when we want a slice of the action,' he says. 'We:

- interrupt the other person, giving our opinion before we have all the facts;
- interrogate them in an attempt to mould their problem into a shape our opinions agree with;
- try to come up with a quick-fix "solution" to their dilemma while they're still giving us the details, even
- change the subject if we sense we're on a loser!'

'Now all of these things are compatible with *hearing* the other person but completely incompatible with *listening* to them. Why? Because listening means that we bin the temptation to turn the spotlight on ourselves and instead allow the other person to unfold their thoughts in their own time and in their own way.'

## WHAT YOU DO

**Put yourself in the other person's shoes**

## WHAT IT DOES

A recent study conducted within the medical profession shows that including a patient's photo alongside the results of their scans enables a more meticulous reading from the radiologist interpreting the images. They're more likely to notice unexpected abnormalities on the scan that may have implications beyond the scope of the initial examination.

Now the reason for this is interesting. It's thought that the inclusion of a photograph encourages the radiologist to approach the patient as a human being and not (as is usually the case) as an anonymous case study. It encourages them, in other words, to *see* what's on the scans instead of just looking at them.

Such a finding, as Andy remarks, makes perfect sense. When it comes to performance across various professions, there's an optimum balance between emotional detachment and involvement.

'The best hostage negotiators, for instance, are able to put themselves not just in the other person's head but also in their gut,' he says. 'But they use their *own* heads to do that. Not their hearts. If you think of the other person's brain as being behind enemy lines, then it's less a case of boots on the ground and more a case of sending in a psychological drone to quietly fly over the fear and anger mountains and calmly feed back pictures.'

Very true.

But apply this dynamic to everyday life and we uncover a fundamental mistake that pretty much all of us make when we listen. As soon as someone starts telling us about something that's happened to them, we immediately compare it with similar things that have happened to *us* … and assume they feel like we did.

But do they? Actually, chances are they may not.

In no time at all we're edging towards the spotlight, uttering words like 'I', 'my' and 'me'. All of a sudden it's *our* show, not theirs, and we're elbowing them out of the way.*

In the martial arts the ancient Zen masters used the word *shoshin*, or beginner's mind. This referred to the profoundly spiritual state of tuning one's consciousness exclusively to the present moment – rather like mindfulness today – integral to which are the psychological properties of:

- *curiosity*
- *openness, and*
- *acceptance.*

Our own experiences *might* help the other person … but they might not. The other person *might* feel like we felt … but they might not.

'In the beginner's mind there are many possibilities. In the expert's mind there are few,' the Buddhist teacher Shunryu Suzuki once said. Listen to the beginner. Then, begin to listen …

---

*We shall be exploring the dangers of the assumed similarity mindset in more detail later in the section on first impressions.

## WHAT YOU DO
**Hold up a mirror**

## WHAT IT DOES

Several years ago a bunch of researchers at a university in the Netherlands set themselves a question that for some reason or other attracted unprecedented attention among their students:

### How, using the principles of psychology, could waiters increase their tips?

One of the strategies they uncovered was unusual to say the least: waiters should repeat customers' orders back to them after they'd written them down.

The rationale was simple. Basically, we like people who are like us … and when waiters repeat our orders, we subconsciously feel that they're more like us than they are.

Think about it. People who have good rapport automatically mirror each other's gestures and speech. So by repeating customers' orders back to them, waiters manufacture a certain degree of sameness with those customers. Which means, in turn, that the customers like them more and tend to leave bigger tips.

Now as we said, the results of this study certainly got the students' attention. All of a sudden, in a certain restaurant quarter in Holland, it took double the time to order your *bieren* and *pannekoeken*. But actually it shouldn't just be the students sitting up and taking notice. It should be all of us. Because, unsurprisingly perhaps, this same principle of mimicry and rapport-building doesn't just work *between* the tables. It also works *across* them. Conversational practices such as:

- repeating and reassuring ('I understand completely why you feel left out. I would too.')
- summing up, playing back and double-checking ('So your main problem isn't with the programme itself but rather with the way it's being implemented. Is that right?')
- clarification, qualification and reframing:
  'Why is that so important?'
  'What do you mean by "acting strangely"?'
  'Why do you think that remark was directed at you?'

… each make the person who's speaking feel validated, understood and empowered in some respect.

- It makes them feel that you've 'got it' or at least that you're trying to get it.
- It makes them feel that it's worth it, that they're not being judged or patronized.
- It challenges them to unpack their immediate suppositions and assumptions in a cooler, calmer, more measured and analytical light.
- It enables the transition from raw, reactive emotion to a quieter, more constructive position where solutions may be found through a simple shift in perspective.

'So rather than empathy-bombing the other person from above by directly comparing what's happened to them with what's happened to you,' advises Andy, 'drop the "same boat" stuff in under the radar and use it, when needed, as a psychological chemical weapon.'

## WHAT YOU DO

Be aware that words account for less than 10 per cent of the communication that occurs when two people are in conversation. Tone of voice and emphasis do most of the heavy lifting. In addition, also bear in mind that around 50 per cent of communication takes place through physiological signals such as gestures and posture ...

## WHAT IT DOES

Back in the mid-1990s, the then Secretary of State for Northern Ireland, Mo Mowlam, was having a rough time. On the one hand she was undergoing chemotherapy for a brain tumour, while on the other the Republicans and Unionists were proving as intransigent as ever around the negotiating table.

One afternoon in Stormont things, quite literally, came to a head. With Ian Paisley and Gerry Adams taking potshots at each other – just another day at the office – Mowlam did something that no other politician would, or *could*, ever have done.

She whipped off her wig and tossed it across the table.

'Fuck this!' she shouted, bald as a lapdancer's bush. 'This sodding thing is starting to itch. Now, the lot of you – bloody well grow up!' Several years later the Good Friday Agreement was born.

Much has been written on body language and the like down the years, and frankly a lot of it is bollocks. But some manoeuvres *have* withstood the rigours of scientific scrutiny over time and proven their mettle in a diverse array of social influence amphitheatres ... from clinical consulting rooms to speed-dating counters to ... yes, even political negotiating tables.

Just ask Gerry Adams!

Here's a simple selection:

1.  **Make eye contact with the other person,** even if what they're saying makes you feel uncomfortable. Not only does this give you the opportunity to carefully study their facial expressions (subtle clues as to what's *really* being said often show up here), it also indicates that you're:

    - *giving the other person your full attention*
    - *connecting with them as a fellow human being, and*
    - *taking things in.*

    But don't overdo it. Studies reveal that while two individuals typically engaged in conversation will 'lock eyes' around 30 per cent of the total time they're together – the average duration of such mutual gaze being 1.2 seconds – they don't look at each other in equal measure. Listeners look directly at speakers on average around 75 per cent of the time – while speakers look directly at listeners just 40 per cent of the time. Up that former figure to 85 per cent plus and it starts to get uncomfortable. A definite air of spookiness begins to 'creep' in.

2.  **Encourage the speaker at the right time** using filler words such as: *yeah, wow, mmm, I see, right.* And don't forget to nod your head occasionally (*occasionally* – again, don't overdo it). Take your cue from their tone of voice ... whether, at certain points, they want you to:

    - *agree with them*
    - *indicate surprise, or*
    - *simply just be there.*

3.  **Avoid clichés – like the plague.** They go down like a lead balloon. Unless, ahem, you're being ironic.

    Phrases such as …

    - 'There's plenty more fish in the sea'
    - 'It'll work out all right in the end', and
    - 'Well, nobody died!'

    … not only exhibit a lack of imagination and engagement, they also serve to minimize the other person's problem. About as useful as … ?

4.  **Employ simple matching and pacing techniques**, such as:

    - Mirroring the speaker's body position and movements. (Andy: 'Allow a hiatus of 20–30 seconds otherwise it looks like you're some piss-taking NLP twat!')
    - Orienting your posture towards the other person instead of away from them. (Research shows that political candidates who move towards an audience on stage when answering questions are seen as more open and trustworthy than those who step backwards or move from side to side.)
    - When you *do* open your mouth … calibrating your verbal rev counter so that your rate of speech matches that of the other person. (Studies reveal that verbal mirroring can be just as powerful a rapport-builder as physical mirroring – if not, in some instances, even more so.)

    'Above all,' says Andy, 'be patient and keep your hair on. Even if it *does* start to itch!'

```
┌ ─ ─ ─ ─ ─ ─ ─ ─ ─ ─ ─ ─ ─   WHAT YOU DO   ─ ─ ─ ─ ─ ─ ─ ─ ─ ─ ─ ─ ─ ┐
│                               Follow up                               │
│                                                                       │
└ ─ ─ ─ ─ ─ ─ ─ ─ ─ ─ ─ ─ ─   WHAT IT DOES   ─ ─ ─ ─ ─ ─ ─ ─ ─ ─ ─ ─ ─ ┘
```

Richard Dawkins, writing in the *Guardian* just three days after the death of his good friend Douglas Adams back in 2001, recounted the following little parable that Adams was particularly fond of.

A man is in deep conversation with an engineer about how a television set works. The man believes that inside each television set is a legion of loose-limbed homunculi who manipulate images with pinpoint, quantum dexterity and lightning sleight of hand.

The beleaguered engineer is at pains to convince him otherwise. Utterly bemused by the man's Lilliputian lunacy – but determined, in equal measure, to 'put him in the picture' – the engineer expatiates on the physics of light entertainment …

… about high-frequency modulations of the electro-magnetic spectrum …

… about transmitters and receivers …

… about amplifiers and cathode ray tubes …

… and about scan lines that pan up and down phospho-rescent screens.

Eventually, when he's finally finished apprising the man of what *really* goes on inside television sets, he's exhausted. 'So,' he says, 'must feel weird now, huh?'

The man smiles. 'Not really,' he says. 'To be honest, I always suspected there was more to it than I thought.' Then he pauses. 'But come on,' he says. 'Just between you and me – there's gotta be *one or two* little men, right?'

The moral of this story doesn't need any explaining. No matter how hard you try to get through to someone, you can never be *absolutely* sure that your efforts haven't been in vain. This doesn't just apply to the delivery of cold, unassailable facts, of course. It pertains to all aspects of persuasive communication, from gentle advice on the one hand to a good old-fashioned bollocking on the other. Which is why a good listener will never leave things hanging.

- A follow-up phone call
- A 'how's-it-going' email, or even
- A 'fancy-a-coffee-if-you're-passing' text just to see how things are …

… demonstrates to the other person that it's not a case of 'out of sight, out of mind' but that you really do care about them.

'Even if you don't!' quips Andy.

'One of the CEOs I used to work with in the City a few years ago had a nice line in that kind of thing,' he continues. 'This bloke was so smooth he could charm the tan off Tom Jones. Anyway, the day after certain members of his staff – anyone in a skirt, basically – came to his office with a problem, he'd drop by their workstation with an expensive bottle of red. "Do you drink wine?" he'd inquire. To which the answer, of course, was yes. "Good," he'd say. "This is for you. Don't ask – it fell off the back of a lorry."

'It hadn't, of course. The wanker was on a mission. It just added to the laddish charm. Then he'd turn the tables on them … act as if *they'd* done *him* a favour by coming to see him. "I just want you to know how much I appreciated you popping in," he'd say. "I learned a lot *myself* from our conversation and the door's open any time."

'You know what, Kev? It used to work like a dream. Everyone loved him. He had the old Agony Uncle routine down to a fine art. Unfortunately, though, that bloke was one of the *bad* psychopaths.

'The bastard was shagging for England!'

# THINK OUTSIDE THE BOX

A terrorist hijacks a flight between London and Cape Town shortly after it has taken off. He gets on the radio to Air Traffic Control and makes his demands known to the authorities. The deal is this. He will get the pilot to land the plane in Lisbon, where he will release the passengers in exchange for £100,000 in cash in a rucksack and two parachutes. With the cash and the parachutes safely in his possession, he will then get the pilot to take off again for an unknown destination.

The authorities give in to the hijacker's demands and the deal is struck in Lisbon as agreed. Once airborne again, the plane subsequently heads due south to Africa where, over a remote part of the Sahara desert, the hijacker jumps out with the rucksack of money on his back, never to be seen again.

The second parachute lies abandoned on the floor of the plane. Unopened.

Question: Why did the hijacker ask for two parachutes if he only ever intended to use one?

Andy thinks about this for a minute.

It's seven o'clock on a glorious August morning and we're halfway across Wimbledon Common on a run. In the spring of 2016 the old boy will be part of an expedition that's walking to the South Pole and he's getting into shape. He's going to have his work cut out, I can tell you. Blimey, if he was going tomorrow he wouldn't even make the South Circular.

Andy's usually pretty good at these kinds of questions. But this is a tricky one and I don't expect him to get it. I must've asked a hundred or so people over the past couple of years and only one of them had managed to work it out. Oddly enough, that was a psychopath in a super-max prison in the States. One of the bad, as opposed to the good, variety.

But as ever Andy's full of surprises. And as we barrel north of the river over Wandsworth Bridge, he suddenly opens his mouth.

'Got it,' he says.

I shoot him a sideways glance.

'Yeah?' I say. 'I'd be amazed if you have.'

We keep pounding the pavement while Andy goes through the options again in his head. When he's satisfied that everything stacks up, he says:

'It's actually pretty obvious when you think about it. It's the kind of thing you really *would* do if you were in that situation. I reckon it's to make sure the security services don't give him a dud chute.'

'Go on,' I say.

'Well,' explains Andy, 'if the hijacker asked for just the one chute, he'd be making his intentions pretty clear, wouldn't he? Once they were up and running again he was going to bail out at some point and leave the pilot to it. Now think about it. If that were the case, he'd be running a big risk. What's there to prevent the authorities from palming him off with a wrong 'un? When it didn't open and they found him in a crumpled heap with a hundred grand still on his back – we'll take that, thank you very much – they could just put it down to a simple malfunction. Luck of the draw.

'But by asking for two chutes he suddenly has the negotiators over a barrel. By asking for two he's selling them the dummy – not that they know at the time, of course – that he's not going to jump alone. He's giving them the impression that at some point after take-off he's going to ditch the plane and force the pilot to jump out with him. Now that puts the security boys in a bit of a dilemma.

'If they pack a dud chute how do they know that, when it comes to crunch time, the pilot won't get it? The bottom line is: they don't. So they have to hand over two good 'uns and err on the side of caution … which means that the hijacker can jump out with complete peace of mind and a hundred thousand quid in used notes as pocket money. Job done. Luvvly jubbly!'

# GOOD PSYCHOPATH TIPS

## Think Outside the Box

Ever since I've known him, Andy has always been good at thinking outside the box.

'I used to work in an undertakers,' he says.

But actually it's a skill that's open to all of us – and it's a lot easier than you might think. Here are three tips that will help you make the leap.

---

### WHAT YOU DO

**Think of every problem as having a solution ...**

### WHAT IT DOES

---

... Every. Single. One. This completely spring-cleans your mindset. Instead of thinking: 'I've tried everything I can, not even Stephen Hawking could solve this,' think instead: 'Well, I haven't cracked it yet so there must be something I'm not getting here.'

This simple shift in perspective is a complete game changer.

'We used to have a saying back in the Regiment,' Andy tells me. '"When you've tried every single thing you can think of ... try something else."'

It works! Why? Because when every problem is viewed as having a solution, anything-is-possible, outside-the-box thinking becomes second nature.

---

A little old lady walks into the Bank of England one day, carrying a holdall of cash. She insists that she speak to the governor because she wants to open a savings account and it's a lot of money. After much deliberation, the bank staff finally usher her into Mark Carney's office.

Carney asks her how much she would like to deposit.

'£250,000,' the old lady replies and dumps the cash out of her bag on to his desk.

Carney, needless to say, is curious as to how the old lady has come by all this money. 'Madam,' he says, 'forgive me for appearing rude, but it's unusual for someone of your age to have so much cash on their person. Would you mind my asking you where you got it from?'

'Not at all,' the old lady replies. 'I make bets.'

Now the governor is *really* intrigued. 'Bets?' he asks. 'What kind of bets?'

'Well,' says the old lady. 'How about this? I'll bet you £50,000 that your balls are square!'

Carney can't believe it. 'That's ridiculous!' he laughs. 'Do you really think you're going to win that kind of bet?'

The old lady stands her ground. 'Of course,' she says, 'otherwise I wouldn't have made it. Now, do you want to take my bet or don't you?'

The governor looks her straight in the eye. 'OK,' he says. 'You're on! I'll bet you £50,000 that my balls aren't square!'

The little old lady puts out her hand and the two of them shake on it. Then she makes a request. 'Mr Carney, since there's a lot of money involved, would you object if I brought my lawyer along with me – say, this time tomorrow morning – as an independent witness?'

Carney nods his head. 'No problem at all,' he says.

That night the governor can't help thinking about the little old lady and her bet and he starts to get nervous. He stands in front of the mirror and checks himself out, turning this way and that, cupping his balls.

Eventually, he goes to bed happy that everything's in good order and that come tomorrow morning he's going to be £50,000 better off. True to her word, the next day the little old lady shows up with her lawyer. She introduces the lawyer to the governor and they shake hands.

She then repeats the bet: '£50,000 says the governor's balls are square!'

Carney nods and the little old lady asks him to pull down his trousers so they can all see. As requested, Carney drops his pants. The little old lady takes off her glasses and surveys the scene closely. After a few moments of deliberation she asks if she can have a feel.

The governor hesitates but then decides what the hell. 'Well, OK,' he says. 'I guess £50,000 is a lot of money so you've got a right to know for certain.' But just as he feels the old lady's hand on his privates, something catches his eye. There in the corner, quietly banging his head against the wall, is her lawyer. Carney is curious. 'What on earth's the matter with him?' he asks.

The little old lady smiles. 'Oh nothing,' she replies. 'Except ... I made him a bet, too.'

'What was it?' Carney asks.

'Well,' she says, 'I bet him £250,000 that at eleven thirty this morning I'd have the governor of the Bank of England's balls in my hand.'

## WHAT YOU DO
**Don't take things for granted**

## WHAT IT DOES

The ability to solve problems when they arise relies in large part on the ability to both recognize and implement whatever solutions are at hand. Sounds obvious when you put it like that, doesn't it?

And, of course, it is.

But time and again the root causes of not being able to think outside the box boil down to nothing more elaborate than a simple creative myopia. You don't need to be a genius to work it out:

- No matter how accurately you may perceive a problem situation …
- No matter how good a listener you may be …
- No matter how clear-headed you're able to remain under fire …
- No matter how eloquent your argument …
- No matter how good you are at any or all of the above …

… if you're unable to recognize a solution for what it is, then you really *do* have problems.

And it's the ability to delve deeper into the universe of possible solutions, to venture outside of one's immediate cognitive solar system, that distinguishes the individual who's brilliant at thinking outside the box from the one who's merely good. That, and asking the right questions.

Talking of solar systems, take Galileo. At the turn of the seventeenth century, when Galileo was about, everyone thought that the sun went around the earth. That's what you were taught at school. That was simply how it was. But 'simply how it was' wasn't enough for Galileo. So he decided to rock the boat.

He decided to challenge the status quo and question what every single person in the world believed to be true at that time. The result, a number of years later, was one of science's greatest discoveries. Actually, the sun didn't revolve around the earth. The earth went around the sun.

Charles Darwin is another case in point. Until Darwin came along, everyone thought that we were descended from Adam and Eve. But after his naturalistic adventures on the famed HMS *Beagle* (1831–36), the young Cambridge graduate began to question the notion of divine creation.

The rest really *is* history. These days even Americans have come to embrace evolution. Some of them, anyway.

Talking of evolution, Andy comes up with another example. Himself!

'A few years ago when Neanderthal cell phones were beginning to develop consciousness and evolve into modern-day, digitally sophisticated smartphones, me and a mate started to question where it was all going,' he tells me. 'What was the next step along the road of smartphone evolution? It dawned on us that one of the things that might happen was that there could well be an explosion in the digital book market.

'Anyway, at the time everybody thought we were crazy. No way, they said. It'd never catch on. People would always want to hold an actual physical book in their hands. But we weren't convinced. So what did we do? We drew up a plan to get books on mobiles, to come up with a software package and then to get all the publishers and mobile telecommunications companies on board.

'Turned out our hunch was right. OK, so we didn't put God

out of business or end up in a Queen song like Darwin and Galileo. But you know what? Because of us, people are now able to read *On the Origin of Species* on their phones on their way to work!'

The following conundrum sums up what we're saying here beautifully.

An ailing desert chieftain gathers his three sons around him on his deathbed.

'I'm leaving you my camels,' he tells them, 'and they're to be divided up among you as follows.' The chieftain then proceeds to issue precise instructions as to how the camels should be distributed:

- *Half of them should go to his eldest son,*
- *a third to the middle son, and*
- *a ninth to the youngest.*

No sooner does he finish his bequest than he dies, leaving his three grief-stricken sons to carry out his wishes as requested. After the funeral the chieftain's sons set about claiming their inheritance, but on reaching the camel enclosure they encounter a bit of a problem.

There are *seventeen* of them.

At first they refuse to believe it. Their father had been an extremely meticulous man, priding himself on his scrupulous attention to detail. But how could one divide up seventeen camels in the way that he described? It was impossible.

For days they try to think of a way round the dilemma but to no avail.

Maybe, they surmise, in the final moments of his life their father had become disoriented and simply got it wrong. It's the only explanation they can think of.

Then, just as they're about to give up on the problem completely, a wise man appears from the desert. Noticing how unhappy they look, he ties his own camel up to a post and asks them what's the matter. On hearing the story he's amazed.

'It's simple,' he says. 'Your father was not mistaken. It's perfectly possible to divide up the herd in the way he intended.'

And then, right there in front of them, he proceeds to do just that. He apportions the camels precisely as the chieftain had specified, so that the eldest son gets half, the middle son a third, and the youngest son a ninth. He then remounts his own camel and heads back off into the desert. Problem solved!

A mysterious character, that wise man (aren't they all?). But how does he do it? How does he pull off the impossible? If you've managed to work it out, congratulations! Not many people do.

If not, here's the answer:

First, the wise man adds his *own* camel to the seventeen to make a new total of *eighteen*. Secondly, he allots the camels on the basis of this *new* total so that:

- *the eldest son gets 9 (half)*
- *the middle son 6 (one third), and*
- *the youngest son 2 (one ninth).*

Note that this adds up to a total of *seventeen* and not eighteen. Finally, he takes his own camel back and rides off into the sunset. Easy when you know how, isn't it?

I like this little puzzle a lot. I like it because the wise man's approach to this seemingly intractable dilemma encapsulates, in extremely simple form, the golden rule of creative problem-solving that we've been talking about: not taking things at face value.

Right from the off, our nomadic genius perceives that things do not add up. Quite literally! A half plus a third plus a ninth do not, as one initially assumes, amount to an aggregate of one (i.e. 17/17), but, rather, to an aggregate of 0.94 (i.e. 17/18). This, needless to say, is obvious after the event but takes considerable detective work – or effortless natural talent! – to ascertain beforehand.

How lucky were those three sons that the wise man came along when he did. Having persisted for days with the more 'conservative' notion that their father had got it wrong, they were on the point of giving up. Yet had they done so, the solution – 'out there', waiting to be discovered – might forever have evaded them.

## WHAT YOU DO
### Look at things in a different way

## WHAT IT DOES

An envelope lands on the desk of North Korea's Supreme Leader, Kim Jong-Un. On the back of it is the seal of the President of the United States. Kim opens the envelope and inside it finds a sheet of paper containing the following code:

## 370HSSV-0773H

Kim's at a loss to make any sense of it, so after a couple of hours of banging his head against a brick wall he decides to show it to his deputy, Kim Yong-Nam.

Yong-Nam can't get to the bottom of it either so he, in turn, sends it off to the Minister of State Security, Kim Won-Hong … who also draws a blank.

Over the next few days the fiendish hieroglyphics do the rounds among the Workers' Party's senior staff. They pass through the hands of the Central Committee, the Supreme People's Assembly and the National Defence Commission. No one can crack it. Finally, after a week, it comes full circle back to Kim who, in desperation, puts an aide on to the White House.

'The significance of this cryptogram eludes us,' they say. 'The most brilliant minds in the whole of North Korea have all attempted to decipher it, but so far to no avail. Its meaning remains unknown. So as a last resort, and as a gesture of good faith, the president was wondering whether *you guys* had any ideas?'

Five minutes later the aide gets an email: 'Tell the Supreme Leader to hold it upside down.'

The art of reframing is essential to everyday life.

Simply put, reframing refers to the ability to shift mindset and flip a problem over, to look at it from a different perspective … something which the boys in North Korea clearly had a bit of trouble with on this occasion.

Of course, all of us engage in reframing on a daily basis:

- 'Every cloud has a silver lining'
- 'One door opens, another closes' … and all that.

But the real party trick is to be able to do it when no one else can. When all the obvious 'ways of looking at it' have been exhausted. Or aren't an option. That's when reframing really makes a difference.

Andy and I are sniffing around the back streets of Farringdon in the city of London killing a bit of time before our twice-yearly air-kissing and sushi-eating classes with a local TV production company when he comes up with a brilliant example.

A few years ago I put a bloke I served with in Iraq in touch with a TV company. He was a demolitions expert in the Regiment and had got it into his head that the British viewing public might like to watch old bridges and chimneys being blown up over their bangers and mash when they got in from work. Anyway one night, not long after he'd been in to see them, he was coming back from seeing this girl he was shagging in some tower block in Tottenham when three giants with machetes surrounded him on the stairwell on the seventeenth floor.

Now, there's nothing you can do in that kind of situation, Kev. So he just got on with it and started handing shit over. But then all of a sudden he had an idea. He still had the producer's card in his back pocket from the meeting with the luvvies. What if ... well, it was worth a try, wasn't it? Chances are these geezers weren't going to be the sharpest knives in the drawer. 'Hang on a minute, fellas,' he says. 'You know what? I know this sounds crazy but it might just be fate. Look, you're welcome to the cash but ... I'm actually casting at the moment for a tough, inner-city crime drama and you guys have just the vibe I'm looking for. Not only that but you actually do it for real! I've had no end of trouble these past few weeks finding blokes who tick all the boxes. So … how about it?'

He hands over the card. 'Like I said, take the cash and fuck off. You can have it – that's already water under the bridge. But how about showing up at eight tomorrow morning in Plaistow and we'll give you a run-out in front of the cameras? It'd take a massive headache away from *me* – and for *you* it could be the start of something a damn sight better than this. What do you reckon?'

The gorillas all look at each other in amazement. They can't quite believe what's happening. Here they are in the process of mugging this bastard when all of a sudden he's turning the tables on them and is actually *giving them something* for their trouble. How random is that?

All the time, of course, Den – that's his name – is keeping up the chatty-man patter … asking them about what they do, where they live, what they watch on telly, who their favourite actors are, et cetera. Five minutes later and he's got them eating out of the palm of his hand. Then he quits while he's ahead. 'Right,' he goes, looking each of them in the eye. 'Tomorrow morning at eight, yeah? Round the back of so-and-so. See you there!'

Everyone nods and Den gets into the elevator.

'I might be seventy quid worse off,' he thinks to himself on the way down, 'but at least I've still got a spleen.'

Anyway next morning, Kev, two of the goons show up round the back of these garages and he kicks the living shit out of them! He has one *hell* of a workout – well worth the seventy nicker, though I'm sure, ahem, he collected a bit of a rebate.

So I suppose it just goes to show, doesn't it? His ability to think *outside* the box that night probably prevented him from ending up *inside* one for good!

When I was a kid at school I always remember the classics teacher (that's Latin and Greek, Andy, not Blondie and Madness) setting us a rather odd assignment as part of our homework.

In the forum in Ancient Rome, he told us, a large stone slab set with a cast-iron ring bore the following inscription.


## TOTI

## E

## HORS

## ESTO


What was it used for?

I remember sitting up half the night trying to hammer out a translation before eventually going to bed none the wiser. Then in the morning, over the Coco Pops, my dad – the bastard – got it in five seconds. Must be something about psychopaths, I guess!

Hint: there's a clue in the description. And remember, the trick is to look at the problem in a 'different way'. (You will find the solution on page 176.)

# NAIL THAT FIRST IMPRESSION

A few years ago I had a student I didn't really care for all that much. He was OK, I guess. But he always struck me as being a bit cocky. A bit too sure of himself. As if he were doing me a favour just by turning up to class.

After finals were over and all the marks were in, the faculty, as they do every year, met to approve grades and to discuss the merits of each individual candidate. Extenuating circumstances. Borderline cases. That kind of thing. When it came to this guy, the guy I didn't like very much – let's call him Rick – the head of faculty produced a letter from the university's vice-chancellor.

The letter stipulated that in the event of Rick's average turning out to be marginal – that is, of it falling on the border between two degree classes – he should be awarded the higher of the two classes, not the lower. He should, in other words, be *up*, rather than *down*graded. And that was that. There was no additional information. No specific *reason* for the directive. The letter said simply to upgrade him.

Which, it turned out, we did. To first-class honours. The highest grade you can get.

I shall never forget the morning of the graduation. My office at the time looked out over a large brick concourse and it was (somewhat unusually for ten o'clock on a Monday!) *packed*. Gowned-up students and glammed-up parents stood shoulder to shoulder with shell-shocked faculty members and decloistered bigwigs in a chirruping convocation of exquisitely adequate small talk.

And there in the thick of it was Rick. Suited and booted with a big fat cigar in his hand. What a jerk, I remember thinking to myself. What a creep. In hindsight, I suppose, a better man might have felt happy for him. Happy that three solid years of long hard posturing had finally all worked out. But I wasn't. Far from it.

You arrogant bastard, I thought. If only you knew how lucky you were. If it hadn't been for the intervention of the vice-chancellor you'd never have got that first. But there you go. He got it. And that big fat cigar became synonymous in my mind with the scourge of opportunism. No, scratch that. With *boorish* opportunism. And would remain that way for ever …

So I thought.

Time passed and faculty business soon got back to normal. A new academic year arrived and with it a new crop of students. Soon I forgot all about Rick. Then one day, several months later, a request for a reference found its way into my mailbox. Yes – you've guessed it – from Rick.

What to do? Well, I decided, first things first. What was all the fuss about that time with the upgrade and stuff, and the vice-chancellor? So I went to the head of faculty and asked him.

The answer completely threw me.

Three weeks prior to his finals, Rick's father, it turned out, had been diagnosed with Huntington's disease – a terrifying, incurable condition that chaperones sufferers on a petrifying, painstaking odyssey of neuro-degeneration.

The first signs of the disease are odd, unpredictable movements. The last – on average, around fifteen to twenty years later – are choking and asphyxiation as the muscles of the trachea are finally brought to their knees.

Then came the *bad* news. Typically, age of onset is late thirties/early forties. And then the *really* bad news. It is autosomal dominant. Which means, in layman's terms, that if one of your parents has got it, it's pretty much down to a coin toss that you'll have it too.

Suddenly, I realized, Rick was in big trouble. *Really* big trouble. And had known he was in trouble in those crucial three weeks leading up to his finals.

No kids.

No life.

No future.

No joke.

Of course, no sooner had I learned what had happened to Rick than memories of his graduation came flooding back to haunt me. The suit. The boots. That big fat cigar. How could I have been so judgemental? How could I have jumped to so many wrong conclusions? No longer was Rick the pompous, boorish opportunist who'd just got lucky. He was a man of supreme confidence. A man who, OK, might've been a dick for the three years I'd known him, but when the shit hit the fan had bitten a particularly nasty bullet and come up smelling of roses.

My newly acquired knowledge of what had led up to that big fat cigar completely changed its significance.

And I gave him a glowing reference.

You never get a second chance to make a first impression.

So the saying goes. And usually that's right. In Rick's case, of course, it wasn't. Once I found out the truth behind the cigar, he *did* get a second chance. But it could easily have been so different. All of us have back stories. We're all just the tips of much bigger, more complicated icebergs. Problem is, as Andy rightly observes, in everyday life it's what's *above* the water that counts.

'You know, I reckon that if they'd had Texas hold'em poker back in Shakespeare's day,' he says, as we sit down for a 'friendly' game with a couple of mutual buddies in a room above a sari shop in London's Brick Lane (ahem, after the last time we played – which would've had the Bullingdon Club shitting their flannels – there's no actual money on the table, just colour-coded jelly beans, and no extraneous furniture), 'he'd have used a different metaphor.

'OK, life's a stage is good. But life's a game of poker is more accurate.

'I mean, no one knows for certain what the other person's got in their hand. A lot of the time you've just got to go on appearances. On gut instinct. Experience. Hunches. Vibes. Tells. If you like what you see, then you throw your chips in the pot. If you don't, you don't, and you're out.'

# ANDY'S TOP THREE
# FIRST IMPRESSION TURN-OFFS

## BEING LATE

'If I'm going to offer you a job, cut you a deal or get you to give me
money, the least you can do is be on time.'

## BULLSHIT

'If you're going to lie, for fuck's sake make it good. You can lie to me as
much as you want. Just make sure I don't find out!'

## ÜBERFRIENDLINESS

'Don't try to be my best mate. You're not and you never will be. Just be
yourself — someone I don't know.'

I must confess that I rather like Andy's analogy – though purely on the grounds of old-school literary aesthetics I still defer to Will. All the world's a stage and all the men and women merely players has a bejewelled, mournfully iridescent ring to it. All the world's a poker game and all the men and women sit up until the early hours sipping Drambuie and diet Cokes and then wave chair legs around when everything goes tits up, doesn't.

At the end of the day, it doesn't really matter. The simple truth is this:

- dating
- job interviews
- chance encounters
- meetings with important people ...

... all demand that we look:
- as good as we can
- as genuinely as we can
- as quickly as we can ... !

... which, given the considerable rate of knots at which the brain ordinarily rustles up first-draft character assessments, is often in the order of fractions of a second.

Andy comes up with an example: 'Let's say that at the end of the day as you're about to head out the door, your boss introduces you to a visiting market leader or head of industry. Turns out that after a day of high-level schmoozing he's about to call a taxi to the station. Now it just so happens that the station is about a mile or so away from where you live. Usually, access to a guy like this is beyond your wildest dreams. So ... you offer him a lift. Will he or won't he?

'You're shitting yourself hoping that he's going to say yes – and that last month's *Viz* isn't going to spring a surprise on the passenger seat – but the crazy thing is … the decision's already been made. It was made as soon as he saw you – within half a second or so of you shaking hands.'

Scary, isn't it? Because Andy's bang on. In so many of the social situations we find ourselves in, it's the answers that precede the questions, rather than the other way around.

Need a bit of help getting the right ones? Then get a load of this …

## HAVE THEM EATING OUT OF YOUR HAND

'In business settings, the handshake is pretty much the only form of physical contact you get, apart from at the Christmas piss-up when you drag someone you shouldn't out on to the dance floor for a few bars of George Michael,' says Andy.

He's right – so it's important you know what you're doing. People make an immediate inference about your character and confidence levels through the way you lock palms. Indeed, the practice is thought to date back to ancient times as a way of showing a stranger that you weren't carrying any weapons. These days, of course, you're hardly likely to wander into the boardroom with a flint-carved hand-axe up your Hugo Boss sleeve.

'A leaked email or two is far better!' says Andy.

But even so, the projective power of this simple, ancestral greeting shouldn't be underestimated. A soft handshake, for example, can indicate insecurity, while the quick-to-let-go variety can signify arrogance. In fact, a study conducted at the University of Alabama has shown a direct connection between a good, firm handshake and a favourable first impression.

And it's not just the act of shaking hands ourselves that leaves us feeling positive. According to a recent study at the University of Illinois, observing other people doing it packs a similar feel-good factor. Scientists placed a bunch of volunteers in a brain scanner while they watched and rated videos of two people meeting each other in a business context. When the initial interaction was accompanied by a handshake, the areas of participants' brains associated with reward processing and positive social evaluation – in particular, the evaluation of others' intentions – were significantly more active than when there was no handshake.

The simple act of shaking hands – done well – the researchers concluded, not only enhances the positives of the other person, but also diminishes the impact of any negative characteristics on show.

1. USE RIGHT HAND

2. DRY PALM

3. STRONG GRIP WITH FINGERS
   UNDER RECEIVING HAND

4. THREE OR FOUR VIGOROUS SHAKES
   FOR TWO TO THREE SECONDS

5. APPROPRIATE EYE CONTACT WITH
   MATCHING SMILE THROUGHOUT

THE PERFECT HANDSHAKE

Sounds silly, but always be prepared for a handshake. 'There's nothing worse than someone arriving at a business meeting who has to transfer their bag or briefcase from their right hand to their left in order to shake hands,' says Andy. 'They should've anticipated that before they walked through the door, before they even entered the building. To me it communicates a lack of foresight and poor organizational skills – not what I'm looking for in a potential partner. Plus, because they've been carrying something around with them for God knows how long, their palms are all sweaty.

'I like people who do the opposite – who take the lead in a handshake. In every handshake you can either lead or follow and generally, in business, it's the higher-status person who leads. But if you're, say, at a sales pitch and you want to create a subtle but dominant impression, a good way of doing it is to take the handshake initiative.

'Start from a couple of metres out. Extend your hand but don't point your fingers directly at the other person as in the wrong context – like in the Regiment, for instance – that can be seen as a threat and the next hand you shake might well be the paramedic's. Instead, angle your fingers downward so you can bring your palm up into your opposite number's hand for full palm-to-palm contact.

'To me, that always transmits an open, honest, energetic vibe – and whoever it is is off to a great start.

'Then, wait and see how the other person responds. Because you've taken the lead and are placing your hand in theirs, the onus is on them to "receive". That gives the leader a subtle edge because it allows them the advantage of gauging how much pressure is applied and the opportunity to reciprocate. Matching that pressure is a sneaky but very powerful form of mirroring that in most cases flies under the radar but which in actual fact is a great way of communicating to the other person that you're on their wavelength.

'Finally,' continues Andy, 'people always go on about the importance of making a good first impression. But actually, in business, it's just as important to create a good last impression. First impressions count, all right – don't get me wrong. But it's the last thing a person says or does that stays freshest in your mind. It's the "take home message".

'Now once you know that – and it's not rocket science – it's obvious what you should do. Never forget to shake hands when you're saying goodbye. If the meeting's gone well a "finisher" will top it off nicely. If it hasn't gone well, then a concluding handshake draws a line under things. It says: "OK, let's agree to differ. The fight's over but we can still be mates. Until the next time …"'

## TOP TEN HANDSHAKE TURNOFFS

1. Sweaty palms
2. Loose grip/limp wrist
3. Gripping too hard
4. Not making eye contact
5. Shaking too vigorously
6. Shaking for too long
7. Standing too close
8. Shaking with the left hand
9. Not shaking for long enough
10. Hot hands

# START WITH A BANG … AND END WITH A BANG!

Andy's point about the significance of making a good last impression as well as a good first one has a lot of scientific support.

Research shows, for instance, that if we're given a list of items to memorize, we tend to remember the first few things and the last few things much better than the items in the middle. Our brains then trick us into believing that because these items are more memorable, they must also be more important. These two memory biases are known, respectively, as the *primacy effect* and the *recency effect* and there's a simple, common-sense reason why they occur.

As Andy explains: 'When someone begins talking to you, you start off by paying attention [*primacy effect*]. But then, over time, when they start to get boring or you start having to think about what they're telling you, your mind begins to drift. Eventually, when they approach the end of what they're saying, you snap back into it and start paying attention again [*recency effect*].'

Spot on!

Let's have a couple of examples …

A great demonstration of the *primacy effect* goes all the way back to a classic experiment conducted in 1946 by the American psychologist Solomon Asch. Asch handed out a description of an individual to two groups of volunteers. To one group the individual was described as being:

- Envious
- Stubborn
- Critical

- *Impulsive*
- *Industrious*
- *Intelligent*

To the other group the individual was described as being:

- *Intelligent*
- *Industrious*
- *Impulsive*
- *Critical*
- *Stubborn*
- *Envious*

Guess what happened?

'The second group thought way more highly of the individual than the first group – even though they got exactly the same description?' Andy surmises.

Again, spot on.

The trick, of course, was that for the second group the order of the words was reversed so that the positive ones came first.

An equally neat example of the *recency effect* comes from another classic study conducted back in the late 1950s. Psychologists recorded a sequence of arguments from a real-life court case – some of them *for* the plaintiff and some of them *against* – and presented them to a bunch of students.

Some students heard the positive arguments first and the negative arguments second, while for others the order was reversed. Once they'd heard both sets of arguments, the students were then asked to reach a verdict. Would the order of presentation make any difference to their judgements?

As you can see from the table below the answer, undoubtedly, was yes.

But there was a catch. It also depended on various aspects of timing:

- Some volunteers experienced a week's *delay* between hearing the first and second arguments while others heard the second argument *immediately* after the first.
- Some volunteers experienced a similar hiatus between hearing the second argument and providing their judgements while others gave their judgements immediately.

| FIRST ARGUMENT | DELAY AFTER FIRST ARGUMENT? | SECOND ARGUMENT | DELAY AFTER SECOND ARGUMENT? | EFFECT/ JUDGEMENT |
|---|---|---|---|---|
| For plaintiff | No | Against plaintiff | No | NO EFFECT: Balanced |
| Against plaintiff | No | For plaintiff | No | NO EFFECT: Balanced |
| For plaintiff | No | Against plaintiff | Yes | PRIMACY EFFECT: For plaintiff |
| Against plaintiff | No | For plaintiff | Yes | PRIMACY EFFECT: Against plaintiff |
| For plaintiff | Yes | Against plaintiff | No | RECENCY EFFECT: Against plaintiff |
| Against plaintiff | Yes | For plaintiff | No | RECENCY EFFECT: For plaintiff |
| For plaintiff | Yes | Against plaintiff | Yes | NO EFFECT: Balanced |
| Against plaintiff | Yes | For plaintiff | Yes | NO EFFECT: Balanced |

### WHY IT DOESN'T ALWAYS PAY TO HAVE THE LAST WORD

Take-home message?

'If you want something to stick in a person's memory, then tell them whatever it is you want them to remember either at the start of a conversation or written document, or at the end,' says Andy. 'Whatever you do, don't mention it mid-flow as that's the point where most people experience a concentration blind-spot and tune out from what you're saying. For instance, if you're filling out a job application, make sure you list your personal qualities in the order you want to emphasize them … going from strongest first to weakest last. The same goes for an interview or initial meeting.

'Rule of thumb? If you're putting things in writing it's better to list them first. Lists can be boring. A lot of people start reading them. But not as many finish!'

## PLAY TO YOUR STRENGTHS

'You know what?' booms Andy, as we scarper out the gates of a posh private school in Ireland. 'It's something that they just don't get!'

'What's that?' I wheeze, contemplating how close we might've come to breaking Usain Bolt's 100-metre world record at any given time over the last few minutes.

He yanks off his tie – Henry Poole, Savile Row, via the Salvation Army, Walworth Road – and shoves it into the pocket of his charcoal, chalk-stripe blazer – New & Lingwood, Jermyn Street, via the Salvation Army, Walworth Road …

'That by the time you're called for a job or an admissions interview,' he thunders, 'most people on the panel actually *want* to give you the position. Give *you* the position! I mean, it's hardly the *Countdown*\* conundrum, is it? At that stage they've already selected your name out of probably hundreds of applicants. They've already put in a lot of hard graft flagging you up as a potentially suitable candidate. What they *now* want to do, as quickly and as painlessly as possible, is identify the best of the best for the job. You don't need to be a Bill Gates to work it out.

'The simple truth is this.

'Before you even *think* about flipping open your Powerpoint and unscrewing the Perrier, they actually already know everything they need to know about you. And … they like it! All *you* have to do is make sure they *still* like it by the time they're going through their notes and hitting the double espressos and you're doing the sudoku

---

\*Andy's a big fan of *Countdown* and is actually very good at it. We sometimes play it together on long journeys. Once – true story – he came up with 'dyslexic' for eight but misspelled it 'dylsexic' and got nothing. Stick pound signs in front of the numbers and he makes Carol Vorderman look like Dot Cotton.

on the train home. Because if you do, they'll pick up the phone.

'And how do you do that? There's only one way. You have to play to your strengths. You have to convince them that you've got something they want that they can't get from anyone else ...'

For the previous couple of hours Andy and I have been drumming this in to a hundred-odd sixth formers at a top Catholic school near Dublin. It's the first time since that bloody hoax call from the Inland Revenue a few weeks ago (thank you very much, Terry Jones) that I've seen the old boy sweat.

'Give me the Iraqi secret police any day of the week!' he muttered under his breath as we clattered our way to freedom down the cheese-and-oniony, parquet-and-polish corridors. 'Tits and guns I can deal with. Zits and nuns? Forget it!'

Despite the sepulchral surroundings, the bottom line we think we reached is this. In training, yes – it's good to work on your weak points. To practise the shots that don't come as naturally – or aren't as polished – as others. But in competition you focus on positives. On what makes *you* unique.

As Andy pointed out with a nod and a wink to the schoolmarms: 'It's your A-list qualities you bring with you to the table. You leave the C-list bollocks at home!'

Talking of A-listers and tables, a case in point:

A year or so ago, not long after *Good Psychopath I* came out, a couple of cheeky chappies got in touch with us to tell us about their technique for attracting women (though they didn't quite put it like that ... and it was something we decided *not* to bring up in front of Mother Superior!).

'Tell you what,' we said, 'why don't we hook up in London on a Friday night and you can demonstrate it to us first hand?'

'Fine,' they said. 'We're up for that.'

So we did. We started off with a few drinks in a wine bar in Knightsbridge and then headed off to a well-known nightclub in the King's Road area of Chelsea.

They were a good-looking pair – let's call them Bill and Ted. And they weren't short of banter either. Bill was a plasterer. Ted ran a fruit and veg stall up the Portobello Road. They could've got lucky simply by being themselves.

But they were also a couple of bandits. Charming bandits, but bandits even so. And their technique, or 'play' as they called it (*not that you should try this at home, kids!*), worked like this:

*Phase one* – *selection*: first, Bill and Ted each select a girl they like. The girls selected are a far enough distance apart so they can't see each other.

*Phase two* – *contact*: after making their choices, Bill and Ted go up to the girl the *other* has chosen and start up a conversation. After getting the girl's name – including surname – and a bit of background information, they politely wind up the conversation and slope off.

*Phase three* – *withdrawal*: they reconvene in the Gents where they trade information.

*Phase four* – *analysis*: they tap the 'intel' they've just collected into their mobiles and access the two girls' Facebook profiles. They then scrutinize the pages for particular 'likes' – actors, singers, musicians, TV shows, etc: the more obscure the better – and select a couple they think would go down well.

Let's say, for the sake of argument, that the girl who Bill thinks is hot (and who Ted talked to) is a huge fan of *Game of Thrones* and that the girl who Ted thinks is hot (and who Bill talked to) is big into *Coldplay*.

**Phase five** – *prep*: in the list of contacts on his mobile phone Bill changes Ted's name to Peter Dinklage (Tyrion Lannister in *Game of Thrones*) and Ted changes Bill's to Chris Martin (the *Coldplay* frontman).

**Phase six** – *approach*: some time later, after emerging from the Gents, Bill and Ted then hit on the girls again. But this time, armed with their public Facebook likes, each of them hit on the 'other one' – the one they actually fancy.

**Phase seven** – *set-up*: after steering the conversation into the general direction of what they do for a living, Bill mentions that he happens to work in TV and Ted that he works in music.

**Phase eight** – *cue 1*: at this point, leaving his mobile phone in plain view on the table in front of them, Bill goes to the bar to buy some drinks. He walks past Ted. As soon as Ted clocks him, he calls his mobile.

Back at the table the girl sees the phone light up in front of her as it rings. The caller? Peter Dinklage!

**Phase nine** – *cue 2*: a minute or so later after returning to the table – and, all of a sudden, a somewhat more interested companion! – Bill then clocks Ted on *his* way to the bar. As soon as Ted walks past, Bill returns the compliment.

Back at Ted's table his mobile phone duly buzzes to reveal ... you guessed it, none other than Chris Martin on the line!

**Phase ten** – *taxi*: the start of a cynically unilateral, inevitably short and ultimately heartless relationship.

If you've got the goods, put them on display. And if you're on display, make sure the goods are good!

# MAKE 'EM FEEL SPECIAL ... AND KNOW *WHEN* YOU'RE MAKING THEM FEEL SPECIAL

Here's a question for you. What do babies do on average two hundred times a day that most adults do just seven times a day?

No, Andy, it's not that, mate.

It is, oddly enough, smile.

The smile, as we saw earlier, is an emotional pass that evolution has printed off for us which enables us to accomplish all sorts of miraculous feats – from the salesroom to the boardroom to the courtroom (sequence arbitrary!) – that would otherwise be beyond our power.

Flashing a smile, amongst other things:

- Convinces the knob over there by the drinks stand that his joke really is funny.
- Assures the pisshead with the face paint and the blow-up doll that we'd *love* to be in his selfie.
- Satisfies the muppet in the dayglo vest with a speed gun that it really was just a one-off and that next time we'll be more careful (to look out for blokes in bushes with speed guns).

Extracting a smile can turn you into a superhero ...

- How do you get a table at a Michelin-starred restaurant without a reservation?

Well, you could talk politely to the front-of-house staff and get nowhere.

Or you could try a trick that one top maître d' told us worked on him and be sipping Château Pétrus late into the night!

'McDonald's were full so they sent us down here. Said you might have something … ?'

- **How do you go on a bender for a week without telling your girlfriend – then come home and make *her* feel guilty?**

The actor Richard Harris knew how.

'Why didn't you pay the ransom?' he asked.

In case you're wondering, it works because of science – ancient, subterranean science buried deep within our brains. Here's an example …

Several years ago a bunch of American psychologists presented volunteers with randomized pictures of faces. Some of the pictures were of smiling faces. Others depicted neutral or angry expressions. Once the volunteers had committed the faces to memory, the team then tested their recall under FMRI* – or brain scanning – conditions.

What they found was amazing.

Not only were the smiling faces recalled more easily than either the neutral or angry expressions, they were also accompanied by increased activity in a structure known as the orbitofrontal cortex: the brain's ritzy reward neighbourhood – the area of the brain that crackles into life when we drink good wine, eat good food

---

*In FMRI, or Functional Magnetic Resonance Imaging, a giant magnet surrounds a person's head. Changes in the direction of the magnetic field cause hydrogen atoms in the brain to send out radio signals. These signals become more frequent when the level of blood oxygen goes up, revealing which parts of the brain are getting the most rainfall … and producing those trippy meteorological scans you see on computers on *Horizon*.

… or, in Andy's case, when the light in the microwave goes off.

'I guess in the context of all that evolutionary stuff you keep banging on about it kind of makes sense,' observes Mr Ping. 'Our brains are hardwired to remember people who make us feel good so that when we meet them again we don't have to waste valuable mental resources being on our guard.'

He's getting there!

But research shows – surprise, surprise – that not all smiles are genuine. In fact, a recent poll of 2,000 adults has revealed that, on average, we fake it at least once a day – with just over half of us admitting to palming one off on the boss. So can we tell when someone is flashing us a dud? Again, the science suggests that we can. And that it's actually pretty simple. To find out how, let's begin by taking a peek at what a real smile looks like.

A real smile – or so-called Duchenne smile, named after the French neurologist Guillaume Duchenne who first studied it in the nineteenth century – incorporates two different kinds of muscles in the face. The first type – the zygomatic major muscle – is responsible for enlarging our cheeks and, when we're happy and we mean it, obscuring our bottom teeth.

However, when we're merely acting happy and we *don't* mean it – when the muscle, in other words, is under our conscious control – it sometimes has the opposite effect of pushing the mouth outwards and *exposing* our bottom teeth … such as when we say 'cheese' for the camera, as Andy points out. But there's another, more 'covert' muscle involved in happiness that often goes unnoticed by those who try to fake it: the orbicularis oculi muscle.

To get a handle on what it does, take a look at anyone who's genuinely laughing or smiling – like the woman overleaf.

*A genuinely happy person*

What do you see? Well, in addition to the enlarged cheeks and obscured bottom teeth, check out her eyes. Notice the 'crow's feet' or 'laughter lines' around the edges? That's the work of the orbicularis oculi muscle, putting the squeeze on them as the cheeks move upwards.

And that's the key that the majority of fakers forget. Sure, if we're aware of it we can do it: scrunch up our eyes on demand. But most of us *aren't* aware of it. Instead, we're too busy paying attention to what's happening *downstairs* around our mouths to notice what's happening *upstairs* around our eyes.

'The ability to differentiate when a person is genuinely happy from when they're putting it on is an essential tool for any successful manager, coach or businessperson,' says Andy. 'Influence is all about making the other person feel as good as you can. And the better you are at doing that, the more reliable your happiness detector, the more successful you're going to be at getting what you want.'

With that in mind then, here are three simple tips for spotting a fake smile:

- Focus on the eye region of the face. Are the eyes closed or partially closed? If so, the odds are that the smile is genuine.
- Staying with the eye region of the face, examine the periphery. Is there movement around the edges of the eyes resulting in wrinkles? If the answer is yes then once again there's a good chance that the merchandise is genuine.
- Study the mouth. Are the bottom teeth visible through the smile? If they are then you may well have a consignment of counterfeit goods on your hands.[*]

*Easy or Cheesy: you decide!*

---

[*]Note that this isn't always the case. Some people have large mouths and will expose their teeth even when they're smiling genuinely, while others don't reveal their bottom teeth even when they're selling you a dummy. To be strictly accurate then, all three tells are best examined in unison.

# THE GAME OF THE NAME

Talking of the feel-good factor, here's another guaranteed, over-the-counter prescription for enhancing mood … When appropriate, don't be afraid to use a person's first name.

Don't overdo it, just every now and again. People love hearing their own names. It puts them on a psychological pedestal, creating the illusion that you're giving them your full, undivided attention.

In fact, research shows that referring to a person by their first name just twice in a ten-minute conversation significantly increases positive feelings.

'But don't stop there,' says Andy. 'If you're talking to someone important, make a point of learning and remembering the names of their significant others and then drop *them* into a follow-up email or conversation. Asking how ten-year-old Daniel got on in the five-a-side or how Karen did in her promotion interview goes down way better than asking: "How did your son's football tournament go?" or "Did your missus get the job?"

'Again, it creates the illusion that there's more of a personal connection than there really is.'

Spot on, Andy – you're absolutely right! Good call, Andy! Er, Andy … any chance you could lend me a tenner, mate?

# GIVE THEM A PAT ON THE BACK ...
# FROM THEMSELVES!

'They say that flattery gets you everywhere,' says my best mate Andy, 'but here's something even more powerful: providing the opportunity for people to flatter *themselves*. Sure, if you go up to someone and say: "You work really hard!" they're going to love it. But if you go up to them and say something like: "I know how many hours [I dunno, let's say] *you tax inspectors* must put in ..." you enable them to tell you *themselves* how hard they work, and that makes them feel even better!

'Why? Because it's a double whammy! Not only do people love talking about themselves – they also love being portrayed in a good light.'

Andy's right ...

But actually, it's a triple whammy! Because if somebody tells you something good about themselves their brain infers – at a subconscious level – that there has to be a reason. And the only reason there could possibly be is ... because *you're* important!

# JUST ... BE NICE

A number of years ago now I showed a couple of videos to a group of traffic cops with over twenty years' experience in the job. Both videos featured a motorist being pulled over for speeding.

In one of them, the offending driver starts arguing with the cop. He slouches down inside his car behind the steering wheel and refuses to admit his guilt. In the other, the driver employs a completely different tone – and a preconceived strategy of persuasion specifically designed to get himself off the hook.

The question for the traffic cops was simple:

*In which of these two scenarios would you write out a ticket?*

The pattern of responses was predictable ... but eye-opening nonetheless.

Of the cops surveyed, 95 per cent said they'd write out a ticket in just the one scenario, the remaining 5 per cent indicating they'd issue it in both.

But of the 95 per cent who said they'd give out just the one ticket, there was 100 per cent agreement as to *who* they'd give it out to!

'He's a jerk,' as one officer put it. 'He knows he's in the wrong. He knows our guy knows he's in the wrong. And yet rather than just putting his hands up to it, he tries to fight it. What do you expect the officer to do? Back down?'

Our mind-whispering ninja, on the other hand, struck an altogether different chord.

'This guy's smart,' observed another of the participants. 'Straight away he changes the dynamic of the encounter from confrontation to chitchat. He completely breaks down the barriers between himself and the agent and in doing so gets rid of the whole idea of "sides".'

So what's the secret? What was it, exactly, that turned things around for our persuasion self-defence artist?

I show the videos to Andy and he straight away isolates four key manoeuvres – a primeval kata of influence going right the way back to our animalistic instincts and the dawn of prehistory:

1.  He immediately gets out of his car – eschewing the protection of his own personal territory and thus lowering his status in front of the police officer.

2.  He approaches the police officer before the police officer has the chance to approach him – the less investment the officer has in the incident (even walking a few paces can make a crucial difference), the less likely he is to feel psychological entitlement: that he needs to 'get something out of it'.

3.  He assumes an 'appeasement' posture:
    - *Slumped*
    - *Resigned to his fate*
    - *Leaning slightly forward*
    - *Embarrassed* ...
    ... signalling deference.

4.  Alongside physiological appeasement, he also employs gestures of *linguistic* appeasement aimed at lowering his own mental status while at the same time elevating that of the police officer:
    - **He admits he's in the wrong**
    - **He finds it difficult to believe how stupid he's been – 'duh!' – to have somehow missed the signs**

- He sends himself up
- He flatters the police officer: 'You know what? Sounds kind of stupid but I'm actually glad you pulled me over. You guys do a really good job in keeping our roads safe.'

Result? He escapes an almost certain ticket and is instead let off with a caution.

'By running all of these programs at the same time:

- **giving up his dominant position behind the wheel**
- **retreating from the security of his own turf**
- **reducing the elevation of his posture**
- **self-deprecation ...**

'the driver immediately convinces the officer that, far from being a rival, he's actually on his side,' observes Andy. 'Which, when you think about it, is exactly what you want to do when you meet *anyone* for the first time – not just when you get pulled over by the fuzz. I know, it sounds like common sense 101. But when you read all the geeky human resources stuff about managing first impressions, it's incredible how often basic human virtues get elbowed out to make room for all that mirroring and cold reading and NLP crap. OK, there might be something in it, but there's a hell of a lot more in simply being pleasant.

'I mean, if you're nice, open, honest and friendly, what's not to like? Whenever I sit on interview panels in the City, I'm amazed at all the little turn-offs I come up against.

'People complain that the coffee's cold. So what? Drink it and shut up!

'People complain about the journey they made or the hotel they stayed in last night. So what? You're here now. Get on with it!

'People slag off their previous employers. Oh really? I wonder what you say about *me* when I'm not there, you whingeing little wuss!

'People arrive late. You know what? You couldn't organize a buzz in a vibrator factory, fella.

'In the end, irrespective of how good a person may be at their job, the bottom line – be it in the Regiment or the City – comes down to the same thing every time: do I want to work with them? And if they seem fussy or high maintenance, the answer is no.

'You know, Kev, in the SAS you could be one of just a handful of lads who gets all the way through and passes selection only for one of the instructors to shake his head at the end of it and turn round and say: "No, I just don't like him." If he does, that's it, mate. Doesn't matter how good you are in the jungle. Or how fast you can get across the Beacons.* It's fuck off.

'Or, as we used to say, "platform 4" – the platform at Hereford station that takes you back to London.

'That said, there *are* limits, of course. Confidence is on a spectrum between sycophancy at one end and arrogance at the other, and the name of the game is to strike a good balance. For me, personally, the optimal position is up towards the arrogant end of the scale. I don't mind a bit of cockiness and assertiveness every now and again … if you've got the goods to back it up. But arse-lickers and bullshitters … platform 4 every time, mate.

'In fact, stay on the train. Don't even bother to get off. It's the end of the line … just turn round and go back home.'

---

*The Brecon Beacons – a mountain range in South Wales where the SAS train.

---

## DON'T JUMP TO CONCLUSIONS

A few months ago some poor bastard sent us the following. Now we're not actually sure whether this really happened or not – though as you'll see from the beginning, the fella maintains that it did. But to be honest we couldn't give a toss. It's such a brilliant example of how *not* to act under conditions of doubt and uncertainty that we just *had* to include it anyway …

> This is a true story. Last week was my fortieth birthday and I really didn't feel like waking up that morning. I managed to pull myself together and go downstairs for breakfast, hoping my wife would be pleasant and say, 'Happy Birthday!' and possibly have a small present for me. As it turned out, she barely said good morning, let alone happy birthday. I thought, 'Well, that's marriage for you. But the kids … they'll remember!'
>
> My kids came trampling down the stairs, ate their breakfast and didn't say a word to me. So when I made it out of the house and started for work, I felt pretty dumpy and despondent.
>
> As I walked into my office my secretary Joanne said, 'Good morning, boss, and by the way: Happy Birthday!' It felt a bit better knowing that at least someone remembered. I worked in a zombie fashion until about one o'clock, when Joanne knocked on my door and said, 'You know, it's such a beautiful day outside, and it's your birthday, why don't we go out for lunch, just you and me?' I said, 'Thanks, Joanne, that's the best thing I've heard all day. Let's go!'
>
> We went to lunch but not where we'd normally go.

Instead she took me to a quiet bistro with a private table. We had a couple of drinks and I enjoyed the meal tremendously. On the way back to the office Joanne said, 'You know … it's such a beautiful day … we don't have to go right back to the office, do we?' I replied with, 'I suppose not. What do you have in mind?' She said, 'Let's go to my apartment, it's just around the corner.'

After arriving at her apartment Joanne turned to me and said, 'Boss, if you don't mind I'm gonna slip into the bedroom for just a moment. I'll be right back.'

'OK,' I replied nervously. She went into the bedroom and, after a couple of minutes, she came out carrying a huge birthday cake … followed by my wife, my kids, and dozens of my friends and co-workers all singing 'Happy Birthday'.

And I just sat there …

On the couch …

Stark bollock naked.

Now as I say we couldn't swear to it that this is a true story. But whether it is or whether it isn't, there's certainly truth *in it*, that's for sure. Our brains evolved to see patterns; to speed-read the script of everyday conscious experience. And as we skim the plotlines and characters there's always a danger that we're not just going to get the wrong end of the stick, but, exactly like our birthday boy just now, the wrong stick entirely!

# Think you you can't be fooled?

**You just were. Read it again.**

This danger, as Andy points out, is especially acute in familiar situations that incorporate novel components. (Were *you* fooled?) Which is precisely the case when we meet someone new for the first time. We're familiar with the *meeting* part of the equation. But not with *the someone new* part.

So what do we do? Well, often, to help things along, we assume that the person shares similar views and interests to our own. We play on perceived commonalities. But this is a tactic fraught with social risk.

'Because actually,' as Andy points out, 'they may not. And if you touch a raw nerve the very first time you meet someone, the discomfort, irritation and general social awkwardness that ensues is administered without the anaesthetic of a previously empathetic relationship to dull the pain. Definitely *not* a good way of getting someone to like you!'

Andy's point is a simple one, but it has profound implications for how we interact with people we don't know. Psychologists, in fact, have a term for the phenomenon he describes: the *assumed similarity bias*. And you find it everywhere.

Here's an example. One evening you find yourself at the back of a long checkout queue in the supermarket. Of the twenty or so bays available, only four are actually manned. You turn to the person next to you and say … well, *what* exactly?

- 'These bloody supermarkets are a disgrace! Look – it's peak time and only four checkouts are open!'
- 'It's quite nice standing here in this queue after a busy day at work, isn't it? It gives you time to clear your head, draw a line under things.'

Chances are it's going to be the first option. Why? Because nine times out of ten that's how you feel! And because *you* feel that way you automatically assume the other person is going to feel the same. But there's always the chance they won't. And that, actually, they couldn't care less about whatever it is that's eating you.

'Which is fine if you're standing in a checkout queue in Morrisons,' comments Andy. 'Who gives a shit? But if you're sitting there making small talk before the biggest job interview of your life, do you really want to take the risk that, yes, while you agree that history is important and offers us an incalculably discerning perspective on the present, "clear history" is probably the best invention ever?'

Er, no.

The writer Anaïs Nin puts it a little more circumspectly.

'We don't see things as *they* are. We see them as *we* are.'

It's good to bear that in mind next time you're in the company of people you've only just met.

Once, as an undergraduate, I was waiting for a taxi outside my college. It was raining, and everyone else's ride – you know how it is – seemed to be arriving before mine. It was one of those days. Eventually a car pulled up right in front of me only for some bloke to appear out of nowhere and jump straight in. *That* was the final straw! Bristling up to the passenger side of the vehicle, I wrenched open the door, hoisted him out, clambered in in his place, and demanded that the driver take me into town.

Turned out it wasn't a cab at all.

But his missus.

I'll never forget the look on that woman's face!*

*Talking of cars and the danger of jumping to conclusions, Ed Galea, professor of mathematical modelling at the University of Greenwich in London has interviewed more than 1,000 plane crash survivors from over 100 incidents worldwide. One of the major predictors of getting out alive, Galea's research reveals, is efficient release of the seatbelt – the problem being that many passengers resort to pushing buttons … as if they were in the Volvo.

## FIND SOME COMMON GROUND

Of course, the observation that you shouldn't *assume* everyone you meet holds the same set of cards as you do doesn't mean to say that similarities don't exist. The likelihood is that they do – and if you want to increase your chances of getting off on the right foot with someone, then doing a bit of digging is often a good idea.

This, needless to say, is one of the oldest tricks in the book in the sales industry – as Andy, like the rest of us, knows only too well.

'Jesus, over the years I'd need Eddie Redmayne to compute the number of car, kitchen and double-glazing salesmen who, during the course of a conversation, have discovered – bless 'em! – that they've got something in common with me,' he reflects. (He's just seen *Theory of Everything* and presumably by Eddie Redmayne means Stephen Hawking. The poor chap's easily confused.)

'This is why things like where you're from, what you do and the game last night are such popular icebreakers. And why God, at least in England, invented weather! They're vacant psychological lots on which you can build empathy. And empathy builds careers.

'You know, several years back I actually met *myself*! I'd just done a talk in your old neck of the woods – at the Cambridge union – and was sitting on my own in the bar of this restaurant when a bloke waltzes in with a couple of dolly birds on his arm. Fuck knows what coked-up bollocks he'd been spouting off to them beforehand, but he sits down at the table next to me with one of those cheap, fat bottles of rosé and strikes up a conversation about how he used to be in the army and is now a writer. "Of course," he goes, "a lot of what I did I can't talk about. I'm, er, Andy McNab ... you may have heard of me?"

'Yeah,' I whispered in his ear. 'I have. You're a knob!'

The power of the similarity principle has been documented scientifically. Consider, for a moment, the following.

You go to a DIY store to buy some paint for your lounge. As you enter the store, two people come up to you and attempt to persuade you to switch to another brand. Each begins by asking you how many pots you intend to buy. You reply four.

On hearing this, both inform you that their brand is better. Then one tells you that they've just bought four pots of it. The other, eighty.

Question: in which of these two scenarios do you think you'd be more likely to switch brands?

Most people, when asked, go for the latter. Which, in theory, seems reasonable enough. After all, if someone is prepared to invest so heavily in a product then they *have* to be on to *something*, right? But as a team of psychologists discovered when they enacted these scenarios for real a few years ago, something very curious happens when you find yourself in that position.

Common sense, it would seem, goes right out the window – and the person whose retailing profile most mirrors your own (i.e. the guy who bought four pots) becomes the more persuasive.

The sense of something – *anything* – in common prevails.

Similarity wins the day!

# KEEP THEM GUESSING

There are TWO GOLDEN RULES in life:

## 1. NEVER TELL ANYONE EVERYTHING YOU KNOW...

Yeah, OK, it's an old one. But it's also a good one. Because a recent study shows that keeping someone guessing about what you think of them elevates their impression of you!

Not convinced? Need more info? Here's what happened ...

A bunch of female undergrads were each told that four male students had viewed their Facebook profiles and had rated how much they wanted to get to know them a little better. The women were then shown four fictitious Facebook profiles of attractive male students and divided into three groups:

- One group was told that these were the profiles of the four students who'd given them the highest ratings.
- One group was told that they were the profiles of the four students who'd given them average ratings.
- Women in the third group were told that it wasn't known how much each of the students liked them.

After they'd viewed the profiles, all the women then rated the four guys for attractiveness. The results were a blast. Sure, the girls liked the guys more when they thought the guys liked *them* more.

No surprises there.

But the girls who liked the guys most of all were the girls who *didn't know* what those guys thought of them. Why?

'Because,' as Andy rightly observes, 'they couldn't get them out of their heads! They kept wondering to themselves what those blokes thought of them … and so thought of *them* more than they thought of the others!'

He loves me …

He loves me not …

Or, as Andy points out:

'It's not so much playing hard to get that does the business for you. It's playing hard to read!'

# GET INSIDE THEIR HEADS

A student who wrote to us after reading *Good Psychopath I* uses a related thought-insertion technique to land holiday jobs.

It's clever. *Very* clever. And Neil, it doesn't surprise us one bit, mate, that you're rarely out of pocket! Here's what he told us:

> The 'trick' is to 'get in' before the interview starts and to implant in the mind of the interviewer the thought that the job is already yours.
>
> 'Let's say that I'm offered the position,' I typically ask the panel at the beginning of the interview. 'What, precisely, do I have to do? The description sounds really interesting. Walk me through it from the minute I come through the door in the morning to the minute I go home at night.'

Nice. Note how the question is framed: the clever use of the present tense. And note how by answering it the interviewer unconsciously rehearses the *eventuality of* – and thereby unwittingly strengthens their *commitment to* – the candidate being successful.

'Of course, as well as being a devious bastard,' comments Andy, 'what Neil's also doing here is simply connecting with the interviewer – the best, and by far the easiest way of making a good first impression.'

He's:

- acting professional
- showing he's interested
- asking the right questions, and, no doubt
- showing off his black belt in social skills by engaging

in the right kind of non-verbal communication while
the interviewer's talking:

nodding at the correct times

making appropriate eye contact*

sitting upright and alert in his chair

keeping his hands and feet still

'Which is brilliant. While *they're* selling to *him*, *he's* selling to *them* … but all the time, unbeknownst to them, it's insider trading! 'Jesus, Kev, did you get his number … ?'

---

*In animals, as well as humans, prolonged eye contact is often interpreted as threatening and frequently leads to conflict. Conversely, the propensity to *disengage* from eye contact is generally perceived as an appeasement signal. A wealth of empirical – not to mention anecdotal! – evidence corroborates such observations. Andy: 'One of the Regiment lads once brushed up on his medical skills by working with closed-head injuries in the A&E ward of a hospital near Hereford. Once they'd regained consciousness, it was standard procedure to ask patients what the last thing they remembered was. Not infrequently – yep, you guessed it – it was some variation on: "Who the fuck do you think you're looking at?"' Another study revealed that when researchers on motorbikes stared at motorists at traffic lights the motorists tended to move off more rapidly – while others have found that newcomers to a work table who are greeted with a long stare interpret such a signal as an indication that they're not welcome.

# BRAG = DRAG

Don't blow your own trumpet. Ever! In fact, when possible, do precisely the opposite: give credit where credit's due. This shows:

- You're a team player.
- You're not going to bask in other people's successes.
- You're not going to nick ideas off people and run away with them.

Bragging comes in two brands.

If you want to make a good impression you're best advised to steer well clear of both of them.

### 1. Drawing attention to your standout qualities

*Andy*: 'If you *can't* back it up, it's going to look like you're full of shit. If you *can* back it up, you're just going to look like a dick. It's LOSE–LOSE. So why bother?'

### 2. Drawing attention to something you've done

*Andy*: 'I'm not interested in what people have done. I get this in business all the time ... blokes coming up to me telling me about some award they won or about some product they launched or project they got off the ground. Big fucking deal! You know what *I'm* looking for? What they're going to do next!

'You can talk all you like about what you've done. But it's done. Gone. In the past. You know what, Kev? People say that in business you're only as good as your last deal. But I say that's bollocks! In business, mate, you're only as good as your next one.'

## TRY NOT TO DROP ONE

'The trouble with you, Norman,' one listener complained to the late Conservative MP Norman St John-Stevas (later Lord St John of Fawsley), 'is that you're such a compulsive name dropper.'

'You know what?' came the reply. 'The Queen said exactly the same thing to me yesterday.'

Just … DON'T.

OK?

# FIRST IMPRESSIONS ... AT A GLANCE

Earlier this year the British Psychological Society trawled the literature on impression formation and came up with a collection of some of its more interesting findings. Here in abridged form – and in no particular order – is my top ten:

### Finding 1: People who make more eye contact are perceived as more intelligent ...

... and people who make less eye contact are thought to be hiding something.

But as we've seen, don't overdo it. You might cop a right-hander!

### Finding 2: Men with brown eyes are perceived as more dominant

But it's not necessarily because their eyes are brown. It's because brown iris colour tends to accompany other facial features associated with the perception of dominance (e.g. broader, bigger chins; bigger noses; eyes closer together and larger eyebrows) more often than blue iris colour.

'What about black eyes?' asks Andy.

### Finding 3: Faster speakers are seen as more competent

Just a 30 per cent slowdown in your normal rate of speaking can make you appear less trustworthy and persuasive. Want us to repeat that ... ?

### Finding 4: The smarter you dress, the more confident and successful others see you as

Men wearing bespoke suits come out on top against men wearing off-the-peg suits ... and job candidates in any kind of suit are seen as being higher earners and more likely to gain promotion than their more casual counterparts.

Who would've believed it?

### Finding 5: Designer labels make you more persuasive

More specifically, they make you:

- appear wealthier and of higher status,
- more likely to be given a job,
- better at getting strangers to fill in a questionnaire,
- better at getting people to donate to good causes.

So, chuggers – the secret's out!

### Finding 6: You really can tell what a person's like from their shoes!

- More agreeable people tend to wear shoes that are practical and affordable (they don't go in for pointy toes and brand visibility).
- Socially anxious people tend to keep their shoes in extremely good nick (overcompensating for the possibility of rejection, perhaps?).
- Wealthier people go more for style.

Hmm … didn't we already know that?

### Finding 7: If you have multiple facial piercings you're perceived as less intelligent …

… at least, that's what some research has shown. Other research, in contrast, has shown that the more facial piercings a woman has, the more artistic and creative she's perceived.

*Andy*: 'A woman came up to me at a book signing once and told me she'd had her nipple pierced.'

*Me*: 'Really? What do you say to that?'

*Andy*: 'There's only one thing you *can* say to that: I don't believe you!'

### Finding 8: Women with more tattoos are seen as more promiscuous

… and also as heavier drinkers!

Studies reveal that men are more likely to go up to a woman lying on a beach if she has a tattoo on her back – and to do so more quickly.

And they say that beauty's only skin deep …

### Finding 9: Men with shaved heads are seen as more dominant …

… at least, that is, in one experiment, which involved photoshopping different hairstyles on to pictures.

The shaven-headed male alter egos were also seen as being 'taller and stronger than their authentic selves'. Especially, ahem, among Millwall fans when shaving revealed a West Ham tattoo …

### Finding 10: A handshake is a reliable indicator of how conscientious you are

Rationale? Like any complex behaviour, the rules of a good handshake must be learned – and the personality trait of conscientiousness* is an accurate predictor of how serious you might be about mastering such behaviours … and, of course, of how diligent you might be at your job!

---

*Conscientiousness, as we saw earlier, is one of the so-called Big Five personality components. The other four components, if you recall, are: extraversion, openness to experience, neuroticism and agreeableness.

As we saw earlier, a decent handshake requires a passable working knowledge of prevailing social norms plus some degree of interpersonal coordination. OK, it might not be rhythmic gymnastics. But then again, it's not exactly trivial either.

'Either way,' as Andy points out, 'you've got absolutely no excuses!'

# SHARPEN UP YOUR PERSUASION SKILLS

Who's the first person that springs to mind when you think of a great persuader?

*Winston Churchill*: 'Never, never, never, never give up …'?
*Martin Luther King Jr*: 'I have a dream …'?
*Nelson Mandela*: 'It always seems impossible until it's done'?

Whoever it is, their golden words have stood the test of time not only because they were uttered at crucial points in history but also because of their gravitas. They convey power, vision and passion … with masses of conviction yet seemingly minimal effort.

'The most successful politician,' Teddy Roosevelt once observed, 'is he who says what the people are thinking most often in the loudest voice.'

Churchill, King and Mandela would not have disagreed. Of course, what goes for politicians also goes for the rest of us. OK, so not everyone possesses the oratorical skills of an influence ninja like Churchill. But who cares?

Whether you're the head of state, the CEO of a FTSE 250 multinational, the chair of a small non-profit organization, the manager of a local five-a-side football team, or a busy parent trying to make ends meet, you've got to be able to harness the authority of language – its vast reserves of untapped natural resources – and use it as a basis of sustainable and renewable energy to impose your will on others. To get what you want done, done.

'After all,' as Andy points out, 'if we hadn't started talking in the first place, we'd still be clobbering each other over the head with clubs every time an email went astray, wouldn't we?'

Er, yeah. Kind of, Andy.

You need to be able to inspire people. To motivate them to change. To challenge old viewpoints and open them up to the potential of new opportunities. And you need to be flexible and keep your influence options open.

At times you have to be clinical. To have a nose for small print and detail. You have to present facts, figures, data … use logic and the voice of reason.

At others you have to tell stories. Be ready with a quick one-liner. You have to raise smiles, eyebrows … use shock tactics and the power of surprise.

Last summer, not long after *Good Psychopath I* had come out, Andy and I found ourselves sitting in front of a high-powered board in the City. The CEO was a huge fan of the book and wanted to throw a big chunk of cash at us to do some work with his senior staff. At the end of the interview the bastard bowled us a bouncer.

'So,' he barked, his cold, hard eyes boring into ours. 'Why should I give you the money?'

Christ, I thought.

But Andy didn't flinch.

'Do you want the short answer or the long answer?' he inquired.

'Short,' snapped the CEO.

'Because we'll make a difference,' replied Andy.

The CEO nodded and the room fell unnervingly silent.

'OK,' he said, clearing his throat. 'So … just out of interest, what's the long version?'

Andy remained emotionless.

'Because,' he articulated super-slowly, 'we'll-make-a-fucking-difference.'

I spat out the San Pellegrino.

Well that's that then, I thought. Foom! … next month's trip to Savile Row gone up in smoke.

But I couldn't have been more wrong. Two weeks later our programme was up and running … and two *months* later we saw a 30 per cent hike in productivity.

# GOOD PSYCHOPATH TIPS

Do you want to hit a six off a ball like that … instead of being bowled middle stump? Do you, like Andy, want to be able to open people's hearts, open people's minds, open people's cheque books without even breaking sweat?

If the answer is yes to any or all of the above, then here are a few things you might want to bear in mind.

The Stones were right.

You can't always get what you want.

But by developing your powers of persuasion you can certainly increase your chances …

# PRACTICE!

Here's a question for you:

How many times a day do you think someone tries to persuade you? From the moment you get up in the morning to the moment your head hits the pillow again in the evening. Twenty? Forty? Sixty, maybe?

That's what most people say when asked this question. But the answer may surprise you.

In fact, it's close to four hundred!

Comes as a bit of a shock when you first hear it, doesn't it?

But let's go through the options. Tot up those persuasion calories.

Well, it starts before we've even got out of bed in the morning with the radio alarm clock. Then there's your drive to work and all those traffic signs. Then there's your boss. Your clients. Your friends. Your family. Your colleagues. The TV. The radio. The internet. All those ads you see above the shops on the high street.

And believe you me – we haven't even started yet.

Here's a crazy stat for you. The brains of modern-day western city-dwellers like us take in as much information during the course of a twenty-four-hour period as the brains of those who lived in rural medieval Britain would've taken in … during the course of an entire lifetime! Scary, isn't it? And you know what? It's information like this, it's persuasion like this, that keeps society cohesive. That keeps us all, pretty much, on the straight and narrow.

Imagine that we were to rig up an alternative society in which *coercion* rather than persuasion was the name of the game.

Imagine, for instance, if every time we drove past a speed camera at ninety it didn't just flash at us and take our pictures but some state-sponsored sensor riddled our fuel tank with high-velocity rounds. Or if every time we didn't buy a doner from the vendor on the street corner he came pelting after us down the road with a kebab skewer.

Not very pleasant, is it?

And not very possible.

Persuasion is what keeps us alive.

But now ask yourself a different kind of question:

- **How many times a day do *I* try to persuade someone to do something?**
- **How many times a day do *I* try to talk others round?**
- **How many times a day do *I* send my words into battle?**

If the answer is … well, not very often, then you're not alone. In fact, I'd guess you were in the majority. There are millions of people like you who don't want to rock the boat. Who just can't be arsed with the hassle. Who prefer a quiet life.

And yet, you know what? You're exactly the kind of people who want to be better persuaders! Who ask us how it's done.

Well, our answer is plain and simple:

'Get out there,' as Andy rather politely puts it, 'and start fucking persuading! Because here's the deal. The biggest reason you *can't* is because you *don't*.'

I have to say, Andy's spot on (though perhaps, on reflection, he's no great loss to the counselling profession). Let me elevate the tone a little here and bring the Ancient Greeks into this for a moment.

'We are what we repeatedly do,' Aristotle once said. 'Excellence, then, is not an act, but a habit—'

'In other words: start fucking persuading!' Andy booms again.

He's on a roll. 'I mean, who knows how good you are? *You* certainly don't because you haven't given yourself the chance to find out. In the Regiment we used to say that you needed two things to be an SAS soldier.

'You need SKILL. But you also need ATTITUDE. If you don't have the attitude, then the skill is useless. But if you *do* have the attitude, then there's always the chance the skill will come with practice. Attitude is all important.

'OK, so you might have to go out of your comfort zone every now and then. But so what?

'Being a good all-round persuader is a bit like being a good all-round golfer. You need to know how to play every shot, use every club, depending on the situation. And you need to take risks. For every shot that lands just short of the hole, there'll be another that lands in the bunker.

'Humour, assertiveness, cheek, the softly-softly approach all have their uses and it's pretty rare that you find someone equally brilliant at all of them. Everyone's got weaknesses in their personality just like every golfer – even Rory McIlroy – has got weaknesses in their game.

'To be a good persuader you need to identify them. Home in on them. Work on them. Take a look at yourself: your body language; the way you speak; the messages you send out. Set yourself little persuasion exercises that enable you to chisel away at each one and perfect your craft. And then, at the end of the day, evaluate how you got on. You know, things get better just by paying attention to them.

'Think back to when you were learning to drive, Kev, and just couldn't get reversing around a corner – sorry, bad example, scratch that! – just couldn't get the clutch right. Second nature now, isn't it? But there's a trick to persuasion, mate – and it's well worth remembering. All the time you're doing it, it's important to keep in mind precisely what it is you want to achieve. And to stick to that mission in the heat of the moment when emotions are running high.

'Because a lot of the time there comes a point in the argument or whatever when persuasion ceases to be about what we really want and becomes, instead, all about winning. About imposing our will on others no matter what. That's why psychopaths like me have an advantage. I never get emotional.

'And that, of course, makes my missus – *especially* my missus – even *more* emotional!

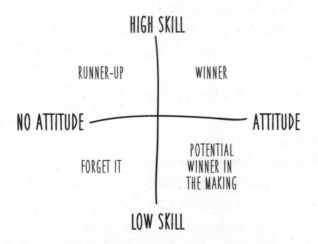

TAKE WHAT YOU'VE GOT — NOW ... HAVE YOU GOT WHAT IT TAKES?

'Want to get a refund?
'Want to get an upgrade?

'Want that bloke opposite to turn his bloody music down?
'Then keep a persuasion diary!

- *Set yourself a challenge.*
- *Pencil it in.*
- *Have a bash at it.*
- *And then keep a note of how it went ...*

> *What you did right*
> *What you did wrong*
> *What went well*
> *What could've gone better*

'Practise your persuasion swing on the influence driving range!

'To help loosen up you can also do other stuff, too. For instance:

- **Monday: tell a joke or a funny story about yourself**
- **Tuesday: give someone some constructive criticism**
- **Wednesday: pay someone a random compliment** (someone who you don't know but fancy is always a good one)
- **Thursday: complain about something**
- **Friday: ask a favour**
- **Saturday: say no**
- **Sunday: smile and say hello to someone** ... just because you can!

'Basically, Kev, if you want to be a better persuader, you've just got to toughen up and work at it.'

My old man would've given Andy a run for his money in the persuasion stakes. The conniving bastard was one of the best in the business. And, of course, another psychopath! He was so full of shit that on his long walk to freedom I wouldn't have put it past him to have got old Nelson Mandela to turn back round.

Yep, he was that good!

As a kid I often wondered where it all came from. So one day, when we were out shopping, I asked him.

'Watch and learn,' he said, and without batting an eye walked up to a nearby parking attendant who'd just pulled his pad out of his pocket.

For the next three or four minutes I stood there like a gormless twat as Dad gave it the full Del Boy and remonstrated with the traffic warden to put it away again. We got the whole nine yards:

- **How Mum had been taken ill in the supermarket. (She'd pegged it the year before and it'd had nothing to do with a supermarket.)**
- **How he'd once been a traffic warden himself 'up north' (er, Finsbury Park?) and knew the score.**
- **How the car (cue stage whisper) was actually a surprise present for me for when I passed my driving test next week – and slapping a ticket on it before I'd even got behind the wheel wasn't exactly the vehicular coming of age he'd had in mind (real babe magnets, those Austin Allegros).**

Eventually the poor old bugger relented and, sticking his pen back behind his ear, shot me a sheepish, anticipatory grin before sloping off in the direction of a builder's van that was parked up in a bus lane.

Dad wandered back over, took out a Hamlet cigar and lit up. Water off a duck's back.

'Nice one, mate,' he called out after the warden. 'Very much appreciated. And you know what? I bet the bloke whose car it is will appreciate it even more!'

## KNOW THE LIMITS: WHEN TO START, WHEN TO STOP ... AND HOW FAR TO PUSH IT

*The Last Supper* by Leonardo da Vinci (or if you're talking to Andy, DiCaprio) is one of the most celebrated works of art this side of Hollywood Boulevard. But why? Sure, the old boy certainly had a knack for slapping oil on canvas. No question about it. But so did a lot of others. And there's a heck of a lot of *Last Supper*s knocking about out there that could, on the basis of technical mastery alone, give da Vinci's a run for its money. So what's the deal? If it's not pound-for-pound precision, if it's not the footfall of dauntless, deific brush strokes, then what is it exactly?

The answer, it emerges, is timing.

Let's take a look at the supporting cast. Pretty much without exception, every artist either before or since Leonardo who's nailed *The Last Supper* (no pun intended) has done so by capturing one or other of those profound transcendental cameos enshrined within its unfolding. Jesus breaking the bread ... Washing his disciples' feet ... Thirteen togaed-up hipsters all sitting mindfully along the same side of the table (what's all *that* about?) like some redbrick university chess team from 1972 ...

But Leonardo, by contrast, goes a different route.

Far from depicting a beau monde, neo-platonic love-in at the Chiltern Firehouse, *his Last Supper* encapsulates the emotional high-water mark of the night: the moment when Jesus reluctantly stretches out his soon-to-be mutilated palms and with reverse messianic hubris enunciates that all-too-familiar bombshell guaranteed to put the tin lid on any works-do night out:

'One of you greedy, ungrateful bastards is going to stab me in the back.'

It's not just the paint. It's the point.

Now timing, of course, isn't just important in art. It bosses the game in pretty much any walk of life you can think of. Including, as Andy points out, persuasion.

'Diplomats have a special word when it comes to resolving conflicts on the world stage,' he tells me, as we nose around the canvasses in the Army & Navy Club's immaculately appointed drawing room overlooking London's St James's Square. 'They talk of a conflict being "ripe" for resolution, of a point being reached where the status quo as it stands is a mutual fuck-up for both sides and political capital can only be gained by coming up with a plan and moving things forward.

'That's what happened in Northern Ireland, for instance. The change of government on both sides in 1997; Sinn Fein coming to the table; the paramilitaries getting a bit more of a look-in; the Yanks, like it or not, sticking their snouts in the trough … it all added up to a positive shift in momentum.'

We make our way to the bar and grab a seat on the terrace outside. It's a beautiful day, there's not a cloud in the sky, and we've just had fish and chips.

What could be better … apart from Andy Mc-bloody-Tab putting his hand in his pocket just for once.

'But, I mean, you don't need to be up for the Nobel Peace Prize to work that one out,' he continues. 'Imagine the barman comes out here in a minute and tries to sell you a couple of drinks for a hundred quid. You're going to tell him where he can shove them, right?'

'No,' I say, '*you* are. I bought the lunch, remember?'

Whoosh!

In one ear, out the other.

Nothing in between, I suppose.

'But if, on the other hand, you're clean out of water and he comes up to you in the middle of a desert and makes you the same offer, you'll bite his bleedin' arm off.'

Andy's analogy is a simple one. But good nonetheless. Many's the time an argument has been perfectly reasonably attired only to have the door slammed in its face simply because it's pitched up at the wrong party. And many's the time a distinctly slovenly argument has breezed by the front-of-house staff simply because its 'name has been on the door'.

Persuasion isn't just about *how*. It's also about *when*.

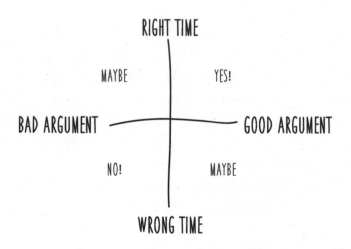

PERSUASION: NOT JUST HOW BUT WHEN

It's basic common sense. But there's a lot of science behind it.

'Take someone who's relocating abroad for their job and needs to sell their house,' says Andy. 'Chances are they won't be open to too many offers in the first couple of weeks after putting it on the market. But if there's a couple of weeks left and they *still* haven't sold it … well, that's a different story.'

Good example. Alternatively, let's say that you and your partner want to go out for the evening and you need a babysitter. You're pally with the couple next door so decide to ask them. Do you think you're in with a better shout if it's:

1.   Their wedding anniversary.
2.   They're going out for a romantic dinner themselves.
3.   Last month when *they* asked *you*, you said: 'Nah, find someone else.'

Or if:

1.   They're skint.
2.   They're big *Strictly* fans and the final's on that night.
3.   Last month when they asked you, you said: 'Of course. Don't rush back. Have a great evening.'

Exactly!

But here's where the science comes in. In each of the above scenarios, which of the possible clinchers do you think packs the heftiest punch?

   • **Their plans for the evening?**
   • **The financial considerations?**
   • **What *you* did for *them* last time round?**

If you think it's the third option – what you did for them – then you'd be right. The mutual psychological force-field of *reciprocity* is one of the most powerful influences on behaviour of them all.

A classic study conducted back in the 1970s demonstrates this beautifully, I tell Andy, as he initiates the early stages of the settling up process with the barman (5ps, 2ps, 1ps … anything not to have to prise open that wallet). Oddly enough, talking about DiCaprio, it was all about art appreciation … or so it seemed!

The experiment was pretty simple.

Each participant was paired up with a partner (who in reality was one of the researchers) and was asked to critique some paintings. Halfway through the exercise, however, the 'partner' would leave the room and return a short time later. For some participants he'd bring back a soft drink. For others he'd return empty-handed.

At the end of the exercise the researcher/partner then asked each participant whether they would do him a favour by agreeing to buy some raffle tickets from him. What do you think happened?

'Ha!' says Andy. 'The guys who got the drink bought the tickets. And the guys who got nothing, didn't. Right?'

Right, I say. Even though the tickets were way more expensive than the drink.

'Funny!' he surmises. (All of a sudden Andy loves psychology! Wonder why?) 'That one simple gesture – buying a drink – completely altered the timing of the request. As soon as they got that drink, the whole dynamic changed. It was raffle ticket season and the bloody things went like hot cakes!'

We take a sip of *our* drinks and soak up a bit of sun. Suddenly, I have a thought. And it's not exactly a nice one. Easy to miss … but a miracle *did* actually occur there a moment ago. Andy *did* put his hand in his pocket (OK, maybe not his wallet, but his pocket). *Now* here we are talking about reciprocity!

'You know, it's just dawned on me that this is exactly why

"good cop–bad cop" is such a powerful interrogation technique,' he blurts out.

'It's really just all about timing. You get yelled at and slapped around for fuck knows how long and then someone comes in with a nice cup of tea and a plate of custard creams, puts their hand on your knee and asks you to tell them all about it. Bless 'em! Funnily enough, it's the one thing in the Regiment that the lads are actually quite wary of. Because no matter how rough or tough you are, it's basic human nature to help someone out who's helped *you* out. Even when you know it, it's an effort to stop yourself doing it.'

Very true.

But if timing your persuasion attempt is one thing, then knowing how far to push it is quite another. Think about it.

'Even if you had Mike Tyson slapping the fuck out of you,' says Andy, 'and Angelina Jolie rustling up the tea and biscuits, no one's going to tell you the full story just like that, are they? No Regiment lad, anyway. So a good interrogator will start off small, asking you – all nice and friendly, like – about insignificant details that you'd probably tell him anyway. They might even say something that's deliberately incorrect in the hope that you'll pick them up on it.

'Think of it as psychological kindling. What they're really interested in doing is getting the logs to catch. But no log burns instantly. It takes time. You've got to build up to that. So first they'll just get you talking. About anything. Then slowly the flames will take.'

What Andy says about tactical questioning goes for *outside* the interrogation suite, too.

In fact, he's interested to know that the strategy of starting small to win big actually has a name in the influence literature –

*the foot-in-the-door technique* – and that with it you can do almost anything. Here's a case in point.

Back in the late 1960s two psychologists in Palo Alto, California managed to get residents in one of its most affluent suburbs to accommodate billboards slap bang in the middle of their exquisitely manicured front lawns emblazoned with the message:

Woo hoo, you might think. What's so special about that? Well, actually, quite a lot. You see, the billboards were as big as their houses and took up most of the drive ... Having them out there was madness!

To help them decide, each resident was first shown a picture of the contrivance by a project 'volunteer' (you got it, one of the researchers) – *where* the thing would go, *how* the set-up would look – and it really was an eyesore. Perhaps unsurprisingly, the vast majority of them (73 per cent) told the volunteer in no uncertain terms to piss off there and then.

And that, pretty much, was that. For the vast majority of *that group*, that is. Incredibly, however, just down the road the vast majority of *another* group (76 per cent) said yes to the installation!

Now why the hell, as Andy asks, would they go and do a thing like that?

The answer, it turns out, is actually very simple.

A couple of weeks *before* they saw plans for the scheme, a different 'volunteer' had turned up on their doorsteps and had canvassed support for a similar pro-social initiative. This time, however, the scheme had been relatively innocuous – a three-inch-square notice to be displayed in their front windows bearing the words:

No one had a problem with that. Practically everyone consented, in fact. It was, after all, what being a good neighbour was all about. Yet how significant it had proven in the long run.

That one unobtrusive request – seemingly unobtrusive, anyway – had incubated a persuasion pandemic; had ghosted compliance to a further, far greater entreaty that presented itself once free will was under the cosh, once resistance immune systems were already irreversibly compromised …

The subsequent display of the mother of all roadside billboards!

As Andy correctly concludes: 'Once they said yes, they had to *keep* saying yes. Because if they said no it would look like they'd gone back on their word … and no one wants to think of themselves like that. In the two-week period between sticking that notice up in their front windows and being asked about the billboard, the rules of engagement had changed.

'In the car park round the back of their brains, principle had started to get lairy, squaring up to practicality and pushing and shoving it around. And in that kind of fight, it's principle that usually wins! Foot-in-the-door … yeah, I get it. And I can see where it gets its name! And you want to know why it's so powerful?

Because no one can see you coming with it. It gives the forces of influence a cloak of invisibility!

'Small request … people think: reasonable. Big request … people think: yeah, OK, I've already signed up to something similar … so why not? I don't want to go back on my word. That's just not me. So I might as well see this through.

'Notice the sneaky shift in emphasis:

- *I*
- *my*
- *me*

'Very, *very* clever! And that's how it works. Foot-in-the-door allows you to take *yourself* out of the influence equation – thereby putting the whole persuasion process on an ego bypass – and lets the other person do all the work.

'What's not to like? *You* get what you want. And *they* feel good about it!'

Andy's analysis doesn't just hit the nail on the head – it gives it a kick in the goolies as well!

'Don't get too cocky. No matter how good you are. Don't let them see you coming,' counsels Al Pacino as the devil incarnate/ head attorney of a top New York law firm in the film *The Devil's Advocate*. 'That's the gaff, my friend – make yourself small. Be the hick. The cripple. The nerd. The leper. The freak. Look at me – I've been underestimated from day one.'

Good advice!

In fact, when most people talk about the psychology of persuasion, the question of when to back off, of when to unplug the ego – of when to acknowledge that the balance of the influence dynamic has shifted just that little bit too much in the direction of personal validation at the expense of facilitating a legitimate, judicious and beneficial change of attitude – is often glossed over.

But it shouldn't be. It's every bit as important as the question of time and place. Or the part played by charm and charisma. I mean, you don't need to be Al Pacino to work it out … If they can see you coming, they can just get out of your way!

'I once remember reading some story about a bloke who used to force-feed his dog castor oil every day to give him a shiny coat,' I tell Andy, as the evening draws in and we head inside for dinner. 'The dog used to hate it. Every time he heard the bloke rattling around in the cutlery drawer for a spoon, he'd leg it and hide. Under the bed, behind the sofa, anywhere … just so long as there was a chance he might escape his ration that day. It never worked, of course. His owner always found him and then out would come the spoon … to a crescendo of howls and growls.

'Day in day out it went on like this. For years. But then one night, something happened. One night, in the kitchen, the dog showed a bit more balls. And instead of running away … kicked the castor oil over! The bottle's open and the contents go everywhere. Up the wall … across the floor … There's more oil in the place than in Andy Carroll's man bun. "You stupid mutt!" yells the bloke. "Now look what you've done – I'll have to clean that up!"

'And he goes and gets a mop. But when he returns he can't believe his eyes. There's the dog on the kitchen floor licking the castor oil up off the lino! "What the fuck is all *that* about?" the bloke thinks to himself. Eventually the penny drops. Turned out that in all those years the dog hadn't hated castor oil after all. He loved it! But what he *did* hate was the spoon. And the way his owner rammed it down his throat to give him his daily dose!'

## ADD A PINCH OF SPICE

For a long time, like a lot of my colleagues in the social influence field, I used to think that persuasion was largely a matter of trial and error. Of due process and negotiation.

Sure, there were things you could do that might swing the odds of a successful outcome in your favour. And there were things you could do that would not.

But there was no silver bullet; no magic formula; no persuasion taser that you could deploy in the middle of a debate or conversation that would wrestle competing standpoints to their knees – that wouldn't just stick the boot on the other foot but would kick all opposing arguments up the arse with it.

But then I began to think differently. I started coming across accounts of a super-strain of persuasion; sightings of an influence that seemed fundamentally resistant to all known forms of psychological antibiotics. It was short. It was sharp. And in many cases shocking …

… with a cognitive incubation period not in the order of hours, days or weeks. But of seconds.

If persuasion bore arms, this would be a chemical weapon.

To this day, one of my favourite examples involves the comedian Steve Coogan – the DJ Alan Partridge's immeasurably superior alter ego. Several years ago, caught bang to rights in his hotel room in an alcohol-fuelled jamboree with a posse of nightclub pole dancers, Coogan, by his own admission, was in a spot of bother. A calamitous own goal looked a certainty. But in a cheekily ingenious manoeuvre he deftly cleared the ball off the line.

'Whilst I was delighted that these young people enjoyed

my company,' he declared, 'I was appalled and shocked to find out they were lap dancers. I was under the impression they were Latvian refugees who needed shelter for the night.'

It worked.

Not for the first time, wry smiles were raised all round – and he maintained, so to speak, a clean sheet.

Here's another persuasion belter of the same hyper-militant strain:

Many of you will know that certain parts of London were very badly bombed during the Second World War by the German V1 and V2 rockets, and one area especially badly hit was the East End.

One morning, after a particularly eventful night before, Whitechapel High Street lay in ruins. As, one might have expected, would the spirit of the local residents. Not so!

On the door of pretty much the only building left standing – a tiny corner grocer's shop – a young apprentice was hammering up a note consisting of just twelve simple words:

That simple note, those twelve simple words, not only regalvanized the spirit of the East End but started to drag an entire capital city up off its knees once word of its content spread further and further afield.

Now at first glance Coogan's debauched denial and the raised finger of defiance of this irrepressible East Ender have little in common. But scratch beneath the surface and you begin to uncover a number of odd similarities. For a start, both pronouncements have a distinct ring of *confidence* about them. Neither Coogan nor his East End counterpart are backwards in coming forwards.

Secondly they're *incongruous*. They're surprising. Mainly because they're humorous.

It's a high-risk strategy, coming out in the media all guns blazing when caught face down in a bevy of nightclub hookers. It takes balls.

Funny, that.

Plus consummate social judgement.

'Far more common, and in most cases far more advisable,' as Andy points out, 'is to maintain a dignified silence – precisely as it is when one's livelihood, and those of all one's neighbours, has been unceremoniously razed to the ground.'

But that's not all. In addition, both statements are also rather *simple*. Refreshingly so. And both, in their radically different ways, establish *empathy* with their audience.

Coogan's dodgy disclaimer isn't *really* denying responsibility for what happened, is it? Instead it's saying:

'Yeah, fair cop. Guilty as charged. But be honest – isn't this the kind of mistake that we'd *all* like to make given the opportunity?'

Similarly, who could fail to warm to the sheer bloody-mindedness of our curmudgeonly East End shopkeeper?

'Wouldn't we *all* like a piece of his indomitable, unquenchable action?' asks Andy.

All of a sudden it's in our self-interest – or rather, our *perceived self-interest* – to buy into the brazen belligerence ... the boisterous, bacchanalian bullshit and concede, against our better judgement perhaps, that we GET WHERE THESE PEOPLE ARE COMING FROM.

Anyway, back in the lab, examples like these I call *supersuasion*: an aggressive, neurodegenerative mutation of hard-core social influence that packs so many psychological nerve agents as to render it pretty much irresistible ... and that incapacitates, with even the briefest of linguistic exposure periods, all known strains of retroviral resistance.

Its DNA, as outlined above, is **SPICE** ...

- *Simplicity*
- *Perceived self-interest*
- *Incongruity*
- *Confidence*
- *Empathy*

... and, as you might recall from *Book I*, the hotter the spice the:

- *cleaner*
- *meaner, and*
- *cognitively harder-hitting* ...

... your persuasion attempt will be!

Of course any instance of high-velocity, high-impact persuasion will, as we've seen, contain a number of these influence 'genes' ... if not all of them. But here are a few examples – from both of us – that showcase each of their effects in turn; that place each, in isolation, under the microscope. Put them all together and you can get, and do, pretty much anything you want.

Andy kicks off with a corker:

The comedian Tommy Cooper was introduced to the Queen after a Royal Command Performance. Here's what happened:

> *Cooper*: 'Did you think I was funny?'
>
> *Her Majesty*: 'Yes, Tommy.'
>
> *Cooper*: 'You really thought I was funny?'
>
> *Her Majesty*: 'Yes, of course I thought you were funny.'
>
> *Cooper*: 'Did your mother think I was funny?'
>
> *Her Majesty*: 'Yes, Tommy ... we both thought you were funny.'
>
> *Cooper*: 'Do you mind if I ask you a personal question?'
>
> *Her Majesty*: 'No ... but I might not be able to give you a full answer.'
>
> *Cooper*: 'Do you like football?'
>
> *Her Majesty*: 'Well, not really.'
>
> *Cooper*: 'In that case ... can I have your Cup Final tickets?'

## Simplicity

Several years ago a newspaper ran the story of an elderly Afro-Caribbean man coming home from work on a bus. Pisshead gets on ... no seats.

'Get up, you fat black nigger bastard!' he shouts at the man.

'You calling me fat?' says the man.

Bus erupts with laughter.

Pisshead fucks off.

## Perceived Self-interest

Caught in a downpour in London's West End I take refuge in a shop entrance next to a *Big Issue* seller.

'Hey, mate, I bet you a tenner you won't buy a copy,' he says.

Think about it! I did. Hmm … five minutes later I've got a copy in my holdall and a broad grin on my face.

## Incongruity

*Andy*: The actors Robin Williams and Christopher Reeve once swore an oath to help each other out during the course of their lives. True to his word, when Reeve was paralysed in a horse-riding accident in 1995, Williams stepped forward to cover any expenses not already taken care of by Reeve's insurance. Less orthodox, though, was Williams' response to the news that the one-time superman would never walk again.

As Reeve lay in traction in hospital, no doubt wondering how things could get any worse, who should turn up but his colorectal specialist?

It was, of course, Williams. Complete with white coat. Stethoscope. And enema!

For the first time since the accident, friends recalled later, Reeve actually smiled.

## Confidence

A few years ago now I interviewed a woman called Linda Lantieri in New York City. For over three decades Lantieri had worked in rough, tough, inner-city neighbourhoods, teaching the principles of constructive conflict resolution in schools and detention centres. Given the kinds of areas she operated in, she'd undoubtedly saved many lives.

Lantieri discovered pretty early on in her career as a school principal the part played by confidence in persuasion. One afternoon – she told me – catching up with some paperwork in her office, she heard a commotion down on the street. She poked her head out of her second-storey window and saw two boys squaring up to each other. A sizeable crowd was gathering. This, she sensed immediately, could turn nasty. Without so much as a second thought – in New York at the time second thoughts had a nasty habit of costing lives – she threw in the paperwork and came hurtling down the stairs.

'I had no idea what I was going to do,' she said. 'I just knew that I had to do *something*.'

She surprised even herself. Jumping on to the bonnet of a car that was parked nearby, she drew herself up to her full five feet three inches.

'When did the tickets for this fight go on sale?' she yelled. 'And how come I haven't got one?'

Instantly, just like in the movies, everything froze. The crowd quit hollering, the fists stopped flying – and suddenly all eyes were on *her*.

But what next? Again, she didn't know. Just open your mouth and let the words drop out, she thought.

'You!' she said, looking directly at the smaller of the two boys. 'In my office! Now!'

The boy sloped off, relieved, no doubt, to have been spared a certain beating.

Then it was the turn of the bigger boy.

'We'll talk later,' she said calmly.

And that was it.

The crowd dispersed, egos were spared and everything returned to normal.

## Empathy

In the summer of 1941 Sergeant James Allen Ward was awarded a Victoria Cross for climbing out of his cockpit on to the wing of his Wellington bomber and dousing a blaze in the starboard engine.

He was 13,000 feet up at the time over the bays of northern Holland and secured by just one flimsy dinghy rope tied around his waist.

A short time later Winston Churchill is said to have invited the shy New Zealand airman to Number 10 to congratulate him on his feat.

But the meeting didn't go as expected.

When the fearless, swashbuckling aviator – tongue-tied in the presence of the fearless, swashbuckling prime minister – found himself completely undone by even the simplest of questions Churchill tried something different.

'You must feel very humble and awkward standing here in front of me,' he began.

'Yes, sir,' replied Ward. 'I do.'

'Then you can imagine,' said Churchill, 'how humble and awkward *I* must feel in front of *you*.'

 # AFTERWORD

We hope you enjoyed reading this book, folks. More importantly, we hope that you got something out of it. As you've probably gathered by now, there are a number of things we don't 'do'. We don't do vague. We don't do 'clever'. And we don't do the easy option. What we *do* do, on the other hand, is common sense, science and practice. Change never comes without a price – and it's usually effort and pain. But neither last for ever. That's an illusion that too many people suffer from these days.

'It's hard, boring and shit ... until it isn't!' as Andy points out.

Take that on board and you're halfway there already.

This is not to say, of course, that change is always a *good* thing. It isn't. Sometimes people who've cracked the happiness code feel that because life isn't 'tough' they're somehow missing out on a deeper, more esoteric level of wellbeing ... and that they've somehow got to work just that little bit harder to achieve it.

They think, as Andy puts it, 'that enlightenment can't just be common sense - it has to be sixth sense.'

Bollocks!

One Zen student says: 'My teacher is incredible. He can go days without eating.' The second student says: 'My teacher has so much self-control he can go days without sleep.' The third student says: 'My teacher is so wise that he eats when he's hungry and sleeps when he's tired.'

Now *there*'s a man who's cracked it!

We're going to leave you with a complex philosophical treatise as old as the hills …

A bull and a crow are standing in a field. The bull is new to the field and the crow, so to speak, has taken him under his wing. As the bull munches away at the grass, the crow picks ticks off his hide and keeps flies away from his face. They are friends.

At the edge of the field is a large oak tree. One day, as the crow is sitting on the bull's back, he gazes wistfully at the oak tree and says:

'You know, once upon a time when I was a young crow, I could fly to the very top of that tree. But these days it takes me all my strength just to reach the first branch.'

The bull looks round, surprised.

'No problem!' he says. 'You can easily fly to the top of that tree again. All you need to do is eat a little bit of my dung every day. Within a couple of weeks you'll soon discover that you have all of your old strength back again.'

The crow is amazed.

'You're joking!' he says. 'Do you really mean that?'

'Of course,' replies the bull. 'Why not try it and see for yourself?'

The crow is very sceptical of what his friend the bull has told him but decides, nevertheless, to follow his advice. So on the first day he pecks at a bit of dung and, as if by magic, easily reaches the first branch of the tree.

Sure enough, a fortnight later he is sitting triumphant atop the majestic oak surveying all around him and feeling full of beans again, just like he did as a young crow.

Then suddenly … BANG! The farmer takes aim and shoots him.

Moral of the story?

Sometimes bullshit can get you to the top ... but it never lets you stay there!